# Beverage Management and Bartending

# Beverage Management and Bartending

Peter E. Van Kleek

A CBI BOOK
Published by Van Nostrand Reinhold Company

**Production Editor:** Deborah Flynn
**Text Designer:** Karen Mason
**Compositor:** A & B Typesetters

**Photographs in this book (pp. 107–111) reproduced
with the permission of NCR Corporation**

A CBI Book
(CBI is an imprint of Van Nostrand Reinhold Company Inc.)

Copyright © 1981 by Van Nostrand Reinhold Company
Library of Congress Catalog Card Number 80-28543

ISBN 0-8436-2209-1

Published by Van Nostrand Reinhold Company Inc.
135 West 50th Street
New York, New York 10020

Van Nostrand Reinhold Company Limited
Molly Millars Lane
Wokingham, Berkshire RG11 2PY, England

Van Nostrand Reinhold
480 LaTrobe Street
Melbourne, Victoria 3000, Australia

Macmillan of Canada
Division of Gage Publishing Limited
164 Commander Boulevard
Agincourt, Ontario M1S 3C7, Canada

16 15 14 13 12 11 10 9 8 7 6 5 4

**Library of Congress Cataloging in Publication Data**

Van Klæek, Peter E
   Beverage management and bartending.

   Includes index.
   1. Bartending.   2. Alcoholic  beverages.
   I. Title.
TX951.V36          647'.95'068          80-28543
ISBN 0-8436-2209-1

# Contents

|   | Introduction | vii |
|---|---|---|
| 1 | Beverage History | 1 |
| 2 | Fermentation and Distillation | 7 |
| 3 | Beer | 13 |
| 4 | Wine | 23 |
| 5 | Whiskey | 45 |
| 6 | Gin | 55 |
| 7 | Rum | 61 |
| 8 | Vodka and Tequila | 67 |
| 9 | Brandy | 71 |
| 10 | Liqueurs and Cordials | 77 |
| 11 | Bar Setup | 85 |
| 12 | The Bartender as an Industry Professional | 97 |
| 13 | Beverage Control Through Standards | 117 |
| 14 | Purchasing, Receiving, Storing, and Issuing Beverages | 127 |

| 15 | Beverage Law | 135 |
|----|--------------|-----|
| 16 | Recipes | 143 |
|    | Glossary | 155 |
|    | Index | 161 |

# Introduction

The beverage industry is a major factor in world economy, a respectable profit-making profession that provides employment for millions of people. From grape and grain farmers to bartenders, the production of alcohol is a long process. Technical know-how and honesty are the two factors that are conducive to success.

I have been connected with the beverage industry as a bar waiter, bartender, food and beverage manager, hotel manager, and educator for over thirty years and have a profound love for it. I deal with a product, but more importantly, I deal with people. Alcoholic beverages and their manufacture and sales have contributed to our history, economic stability, and pleasure throughout the ages.

The Church promoted alcoholic beverages, doctors have recommended them, and governments have regulated their use. People have both used alcohol and abused it, and many people have cursed it. It gives pleasure to many and heartbreak to some.

The purpose of this book is to introduce the reader to beverage management and bartending as a vocation and, in some cases, as an avocation. As with anything else, bartending should be done well and with enthusiasm. Bartenders should work with knowledge, utilize science, and have a professional understanding of the industry.

Well-trained bartenders can be compared to fine chefs or chemists. They should know formulas, the properties of the raw materials, and the desired results of blending the ingredients.

Beverage managers must have an overall understanding of the beverage industry. They must be able to sell a product profitably and motivate and control employees, but even more importantly, satisfy customers.

It takes study and practice to become an expert. Beverage management cannot be learned overnight, merely by stepping behind a bar and following a recipe. Bartenders are not just mixologists; they must understand people, beverage controls, beverage law, and the tools of the trade. They must have respect for the product they are handling. Beverage management is not something that can be taken for granted. If people enter the profession with a desire to learn, they will succeed with dignity.

# Beverage History

1

**Objectives**

This chapter covers the history of beverages. The student, after studying this chapter, should be able to:

1. Trace the history of fermented beverages from Babylonian times to the twentieth century.

2. Discuss the evolution of fermented beverages to distilled spirits.

3. Evaluate churches' contributions to the development of distilled spirits.

People have drunk alcoholic beverages since the beginning of time. No one really knows how fermentation was discovered, but it is thought that berries fermented by being left out in the sun, and people ate them and liked the feeling of euphoria that they produced. We do not know what the first written work was, but an educated guess would be that people wrote down what they ate and drank. The written words of history contain as much information on the eating and drinking habits of humankind as they do the wars.

Dionysus, the Greek wine god, is a familiar name. Bacchus, the Roman god of wine and symbol of indulgence, is still referred to in the modern world.

The Babylonians and Assyrians are known to have fermented honey, commonly referred to as "Mead Making." The mead was stored in clay pots, which guaranteed them an annual supply of potable beverage.

Once people start something, others always try to improve on it. The Egyptians added the juice of dates to produce liqueur of a higher alcoholic content. Other fruit juices were experimented with, including pomegranates. What they were really producing was a heavy sweet wine. The alcoholic content was high enough to preserve it, but for long-term storage they also used sealed clay pots.

Grapes were cultivated before 6000 B.C., and the fruit that was not eaten was crushed into juice. People did not know about wild yeast spores, nor did they understand what happened to grape juice if it was left open to the air. The sweet liquid would suddenly start to bubble (ferment), and the taste would change. Strange things would happen to people when they drank it. Wine was born through ignorance, but perfected with experience and knowledge.

Grains have been produced since the beginning of time, but their utilization for human food took many years to come about. We cannot date the first milling of grain into flour to produce the first bread, but it is safe to say that the fermenting of grain to produce a beverage followed very rapidly. Again, the wild yeast spores did their work. People eventually cultivated yeast, but this took many years to develop.

Nothing held back humanity's inventive nature. Where there was a surplus of a food product, they tried to make a drink out of it. Fermented mild drinks, such as koumiss, were produced by Asian plainsmen. It is interesting to note that during this period both cheese and its accompanying beverage were made from the same source—milk from the mare and the camel.

The Palestinians used palms, dates, and pomegranates for nonalcoholic beverages which eventually converted to wines. The cultivation of many types of fruits for food led to overabundance. These surplus fruits were converted to fermented beverages for easy storage and transportation.

Throughout populated areas of the world, people independently started creating alcoholic beverages. The South American Indians converted "cassava" through fermentation to "paiwari," and the Aztecs made pulque from grain. The Indians of Central America converted cactus, and the North American Indians used wild fruits and berries.

During the Middle Ages, the production of wine became an honorable profession, and the title of "vintner" became part of our language. Germany and central Europe had over forty known vineyards, some of which are still productive today. Also, during this period, people started producing alcoholic beverages for trade and profit rather than for their own consumption. The forerunners of our present-day sherry from Spain and port from Portugal were formulated during the fourteenth century.

During the Renaissance, the Church became the prime producer of alcoholic beverages in the forms of beer and ale, wines and cordials. The process of distillation is credited to the hardworking monks, who found that they could make a higher-proof alcohol for medicinal purposes. It did not take long to find that drinking cordials could also be pleasurable. The Benedictine Monastery of St. Gall was known for its fine cordials. Some of their recipes are still used today. Much of the flavor of the original fruits was lost through the distillation process. The necessity of flavoring the raw alcohol led to further experiments, the results being the processes of infusion and percolation.

The sixteenth century was an age of distilled spirits both in home production and for trade. Names that are recognized today came into being. Many countries would like to claim they were the first to produce a distilled spirit (just to mention a few: aquavit from Sweden, Genever or gin from Holland, brandy from France, whiskey from Scotland, or whiskey from Ireland, all basically grain products. The English also claim their contribution, with rum from sugar cane).

Serving spirits first became an accepted practice in the home and was a sign of hospitality. Early travelers were accommodated at church properties; and eventually inns became places to refresh one's self not only with food and wine, but also with a bed after a long journey. With the advent of the merchant class, wine shops and ale houses were started. They provided owners with a livelihood and the public with places to meet and enjoy leisure hours. Modern bars and cocktail lounges started late in the nineteenth century and became an accepted part of society in the early part of the twentieth century.

The United States has experienced the same growth in the beverage industry and added its own unique stamp with Prohibition and the cocktail.

## Review and Discussion Questions

1. Discuss the early history of wine making.
2. Explain at what period in history the sale of beverage became important, and why.
3. Trace the evolution of alcoholic beverages from early wine making to cocktails.
4. How was the Church influential in developing the alcoholic beverage industry?

# Fermentation
# and
# Distillation

**Objectives**

This chapter defines fermentation and distillation. After studying this chapter, the student should be able to:

1. Recognize the difference between a distilled beverage and a fermented beverage.

2. Understand the term "proof" and the percentage of alcohol in distilled spirits.

3. Trace the evolution of a fruit juice through the distillation process.

2

# ALCOHOL AND ITS EFFECTS

To better understand the alcoholic beverage industry, one should be knowledgeable about facts, not myths. Alcohol is a food substance that does not affect the digestive system, but passes direct and unchanged from the stomach and intestines into the bloodstream. The normal alcoholic content of the average person's blood is .003 percent, whether alcohol has been consumed or not. Alcohol does not physically damage any healthy organs of the body when consumed in controlled amounts. It is unhealthy only when people overindulge. It is not a stimulant, as most people think, but a depressant.

Some people do get physically addicted to its use, but they are a minority. Part of the responsibility of the beverage industry, and the people working in it, is proper control in dispensing alcoholic products. Bartenders and liquor store attendants must know when to say "no."

# FERMENTATION

The dictionary defines fermentation as a chemical change brought about by a catalytic agent (yeast), which converts sugar into ethyl alcohol and carbon dioxide gas. This is simple and easily understood; however, it is much more complex than that. In the case of grain, the starch must be converted to sugar before fermentation begins. Yeast is a living plant organism found both in its natural state (wild yeast spores) and cultivated. Sugar comes from many sources: grains (cereals), sugar cane, fruits, vegetables, plants, and trees. Only under the right conditions and temperature (59 to 68°F) (15 to 20°C) and with the addition of yeast will the non-alcoholic juices be converted to liquid with an alcoholic content through the process of fermentation. People have conquered science and technology to the extent that the process of fermentation can be controlled and a uniform product achieved.

## DISTILLATION

Distillation is defined by the dictionary as the volatilization, or evaporation and subsequent condensation, of a liquid, utilizing heat to separate or purify a substance. The heat must be controlled so that it is possible to separate alcohol and water. This is relatively easy since water vaporizes at 212°F (100°C) and alcohol at 176°F (80°C). Essentially, the process consists of taking a liquid with a small percentage of alcohol, and reducing the water content to raise the percentage of alcohol. It is a step process, as in the making of brandy by distilling wine.

## THE TERM "PROOF"

The process must be controlled so that the percentage of alcohol in the finished product is known. The term "proof" is confusing to most people, but readily understood when one realizes that the proof is always double the percentage of alcohol specified. If a liquid were 50 percent alcohol, it would be designated as 100 proof. The normal, 80 proof liquor utilized in making drinks contains 40 percent alcohol by volume and 60 percent water.

# STILLS

There are two basic types of stills, the pot still and the twin column patent still. The pot still was the original type and is still used today in making many types of alcohol. The pot still has two essential components, the copper pot with a long tapered neck, and the worm condenser, which is a copper spiral column tube connected to the copper pot. With the modern twin column still, efficiency and control are more readily obtained, and it is a continuous process.

The beverage chart on the following page shows the evolution of beverages from their nonalcoholic state to the products used today. In the mixing of drinks, it is essential to know the origin of all the ingredients so that a perfect blending may be obtained.

**Review and Discussion Questions**

1. What is the catalytic agent used in the fermentation process, and what changes does it effect?
2. Define the term "proof," and describe the water and alcohol content of an 86 proof liquor.
3. Is the use of alcohol physically damaging to the body?
4. What are the two basic types of stills used in the beverage industry?

# BEVERAGE CHART

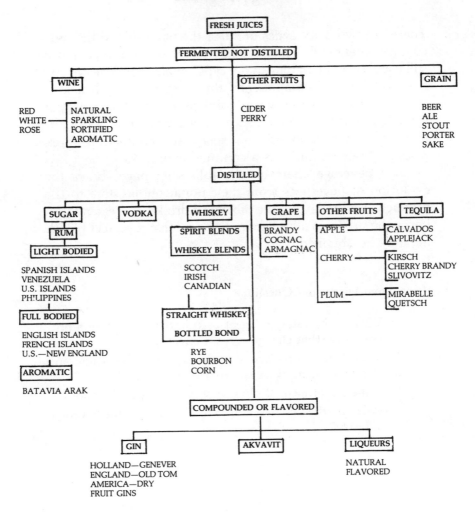

FRESH JUICES

FERMENTED NOT DISTILLED

WINE | OTHER FRUITS | GRAIN

RED          NATURAL              CIDER                    BEER
WHITE ——— SPARKLING           PERRY                    ALE
ROSE         FORTIFIED                                            STOUT
                  AROMATIC                                          PORTER
                                                                          SAKE

DISTILLED

SUGAR | VODKA | WHISKEY | GRAPE | OTHER FRUITS | TEQUILA

RUM                      SPIRIT BLENDS        BRANDY        APPLE —        CALVADOS
                                                                   COGNAC                            APPLEJACK
LIGHT BODIED       WHISKEY BLENDS    ARMAGNAC

SPANISH ISLANDS         SCOTCH                              CHERRY ———   KIRSCH
VENEZUELA                   IRISH                                                   CHERRY BRANDY
U.S. ISLANDS                CANADIAN                                            SLIVOVITZ
PH!LIPPINES

                                                                            PLUM ———        MIRABELLE
FULL BODIED          STRAIGHT WHISKEY                                  QUETSCH

ENGLISH ISLANDS    BOTTLED BOND
FRENCH ISLANDS
U.S.—NEW ENGLAND      RYE
                                  BOURBON
AROMATIC                 CORN

BATAVIA ARAK

COMPOUNDED OR FLAVORED

GIN | AKVAVIT | LIQUEURS

HOLLAND—GENEVER                                         NATURAL
ENGLAND—OLD TOM                                         FLAVORED
AMERICA—DRY
FRUIT GINS

# Beer

**3**

**Objectives**

This chapter analyzes the process of making beer and discusses its proper storage and dispensing. The student, after studying this chapter, should be able to:

1. Discuss the five factors governing the flavor and quality of beer.

2. Discuss the brewing process from malting to bottling.

3. Understand the need for proper handling and dispensing of the finished product.

Beer is a fermented beverage brewed from malted barley and cereals and flavored with hops. Many brewers define beer as liquid bread. The ancient Egyptians and Romans made beer, and in most cases the town baker was also the brewer.

## FLAVOR AND QUALITY

In the brewing of beer, the five most important factors governing the flavor and quality of the beer are:

1. The water,
2. The degree of roasting of the barley,
3. Types of grains or cereals used, other than barley,
4. Quality and quantity of hops used, and
5. The control of the yeast used in the fermentation process.

### Water

The water must be chemically pure and the mineral content known. A water with a high sulfur content would be unsuitable for brewing purposes, whereas one with lime or iron oxide could be used. Many modern American brewers who produce beer in several locations will strip the water of its mineral content so that they will have a uniform product throughout the country. When one realizes that 85 percent of the content of beer is water, one can see the importance of water quality. Small local brewers pride themselves on the uniqueness of their beer, and in most cases it is the local water that makes the difference.

## Barley

Barley malt is made by soaking fine barley in water, letting it sprout, and then roasting it in a kiln. The degree of dryness or sweetness in the finished beer depends on the degree of roasting that takes place in the kilning process. Americans generally favor the lighter beers where the malt barley has not been roasted too long.

## Grains

The grains commonly used in the brewing process are corn, rice, and wheat. These cereals in most cases are in the raw stages, but may be prepared grains such as corn grits and hominy. Many brewers use the term "adjuncts" to describe these ingredients.

## Hops

Hops (the flower from the female hop vine) is the flavoring agent that was introduced into beer making in the fourteenth century. The European hops from Czechoslovakia are considered to be the finest in the world and are blended with American hops grown in California, Oregon, Washington State, and New York State to provide the flavor demanded by the American public.

## Yeast

The yeast used today is brewer's yeast, which is a quality-controlled, cultured microorganism produced under strict supervision. The yeast is the fermenting agent that acts as the catalyst.

# THE BREWING PROCESS

The process of making beer is relatively simple, as most home brewers have found out, but the controls needed to produce a standard product require training and experience.

The first step in making beer, after the ingredients are selected, is called "mashing." In the mashing process, the barley malt is ground to the desired fineness, sieved, and then placed in the mash tub. The raw cereals or grains are pre-cooked and added to the refined malt, along with the proper amount of water. This combination of ingredients is then cooled to extract the maximum amount of soluble materials. The mash is constantly agitated during this operation. When this process is finished, the liquid is filtered off into brewing kettles and is called "wort." The solids are rinsed with water, and the resulting liquid is filtered and added to the wort.

In the next step, the hops are added to the wort as the flavoring agent, and the mixture is boiled for two hours. This process sterilizes the wort and evaporates the excess water. The two major considerations at this stage are that the flavor of the hops be extracted, and that caramelization take place. Thus, flavor and color are acquired at this very important step.

The third step is the filtering of the wort and passing the remaining liquid to the fermentation tank. At this stage, the liquid is cooled down to the required temperature for fermentation. In the case of beer, the temperature is 37 to 49°F (3 to 10°C); in the case of ale, the required fermenting temperature would be 50 to 70°F (10 to 21°C). Yeast is added at this stage. With beer, bottom fermentation yeast is used, whereas top fermentation yeast is selected for ale. The batch is left to ferment for eight to eleven days for the beer process; but with the making of ale, the process would be accomplished in five to six days. Carbonic acid gas is given off during fermentation and saved so it can be added back to the beverage during the bottling process.

The last step in making beer is transferring it to aging tanks where the cloudiness dissipates and the immature beer ages. Some brewers add beechnut chips for coloring and flavoring. This maturing period is called lagering and takes from three to four months. When the lagering is completed, the beer is filtered again, the carbonic acid gas is added back into it, and it is packaged.

If the beer is to be kegged, it is placed directly in aluminum kegs; however, if it is to be bottled or canned, it would be pasteurized to extend its shelf life.

## HANDLING

Beer is a highly perishable product and is affected by light and temperature variations. It should never be exposed to direct sunlight, and a temperature of 38 to 50°F (3 to 10°C) should be maintained at all times. Keg beer, once it has been tapped, should not be held over a week. Bottled and canned beer has an optimum shelf life of six months.

## DISPENSING

Bartenders should have as much pride in dispensing beer as brewers have in producing it. Care must be taken in handling beer from storage to dispensing. The beer should be stored in a clean, airy, dark storage facility at the proper temperature, and inventory should be rotated. In serving beer, sparkling clean glassware should be used. Bottles and cans should be opened in front of the customer, and the beer poured into the glass so that there is a head on it. The proper glassware should be used; the customer will appreciate it. There are six basic glasses used for beer in the United States. They are as follows:

| | |
|---|---|
| Pilsners | 7 to 12 ounces |
| Footed pilsners | 8 to 10 ounces |
| Hourglass tumblers | 11 to 15 ounces |
| Beer shells | 7 to 10 ounces |
| Schooners | 10 to 12 to 14 ounces |
| Steins | 12 to 14 ounces |

The handling of draught beer requires training, but it is favored in many bars and taverns because of customer appeal and higher profits. Draught is highly perishable because it is not pasteurized; however, if the following four-step method of handling is used, there will be no problem:

*Step 1:* Tap a keg only when needed.

*Step 2:* Maintain a temperature between 36 and 38°F (2 and 3°C) at all times.

*Step 3:* Pressure should be maintained at 12 to 15 pounds per square inch. Temperature and pressure are easier to maintain if the distance between the keg and the dispensing unit is kept at a minimum.

*Step 4:* Keep equipment clean. The dispensing faucet should be cleaned daily. The lines and tapping should be cleaned weekly.

Americans have always been beer drinkers. Since World War II, Americans have shown considerable interest in beers from around the world; and various regional beers in the

United States are now shipped from coast to coast. Today, most bars stock a minimum of six domestic beers and two imported. Beer is profitable business.

# BEER TERMINOLOGY

*Ale:* a top-fermented barley malt product with a pale, bright color and a pronounced hop flavor

*Bavarian:* light bodied with Bavarian-type hops used

*Beer:* an alcoholic beverage obtained by fermentation of malted cereals

*Bock beer:* a heavy, sweet beer, dark brown in color, rich in taste, usually served in the spring.

*Keg:* aluminum or wooden container for beer, containing 13 gallons. Most modern brewing companies ship in half and quarter kegs

*Lager beer:* beer that has been aged or stored

*Malt liquor:* malt beverage of beer characteristics, with a higher alcoholic content

*Pilsner:* originally from Czechoslovakia, it is light in color, with a pronounced hop flavor

*Porter:* a top-fermented beer, heavier and darker than ale, with sweeter, malty flavor

*Sake:* rice beer made in Japan, usually 14 to 16 percent alcohol by volume, noncarbonated

*Stout:* top-fermented, very dark in color, strong hop characteristic and fairly sweet taste

*Weiss beer:* made from wheat malt using top fermentation, with a second fermentation in the bottle

## TROUBLESHOOTING CHART

| Problem | Possible Cause |
|---|---|
| Flat beer | 1. Greasy glasses |
| | 2. Lack of pressure |
| | 3. Overexposure to air |
| Wild beer | 1. Beer drawn improperly |
| | 2. Beer too warm |
| | 3. Pressure too high |
| | 4. Inaccurate pressure gauge |
| Beer foam | 1. Beer drawn improperly |
| | 2. Flat beer |
| Cloudy beer | 1. Beer not held at proper temperature during storage; has either been frozen or above 55°F (13°C) |
| | 2. Old beer |
| | 3. Unclean equipment especially the lines |
| Unpalatable beer | 1. Beer too warm |
| | 2. Glasses not clean |
| Sour Beer | 1. Improper temperature of beer either in storage or dispensing |

### Review and Discussion Questions

1. How does the quality of the water used in the brewing process affect the taste of the beer?
2. Define the difference between barley malt and hops and explain their influence on the taste of the finished product.
3. Discuss each step in the brewing process.
4. What are the proper storage conditions for bottled beer, and how may a change in lighting or temperature affect beer?

# Wine

**Objectives**

This chapter analyzes the wine-making process and discusses wines and wineries from around the world. The student, after studying this chapter, should be able to:

1. Discuss the wine-making process.

2. List the major wine-making countries in the world.

3. Draw up a wine list from selected wineries in the United States and Europe.

4. Identify contents of a wine bottle from its labeling.

4

# THE WINE-MAKING PROCESS

Wine making begins with the growing of the vine. There are two distinct types: the *Vitis labrusca* of the United States, of which the Concord grape species is the most prevalent, and the *Vitis vinifera* of Europe. The root of the *V. labrusca* is impervious to grape blight, but the grape produces a musky or wild-foxy-flavored wine. The *V. vinifera*, the second variety, is grafted to the *V. labrusca* root to provide strong, healthier vines. Most wines are made from the *V. vinifera* type.

Wine making is an exact science and, in the case of wine produced for the commercial market, strictly controlled, so that the end product will have a brilliant color and fine aroma and be pleasing to the taste.

To produce a variety of wine, a specific grape type is chosen and, in some cases, blended with other types to develop the desired wine.

After the grapes have ripened to the degree required, they are pressed into juice and tested for sugar content and acidity. In some cases, sugar is added. The juice is fermented in fermentation tanks with the natural yeast or with the addition of cultured yeast. The fermentation process is constantly under supervision and may take from a week to a month. Once the first fermentation process is completed, the new wine is drawn off into holding tanks, and a secondary fermentation takes place until the remaining grape sugar has been used up. The sparkling varieties of wine (for example, champagne) are bottled so the secondary fermentation takes place in the bottle and the carbonic acid gas is captured.

Wines that are to be aged are transferred to aging barrels and held until they are bottled. Water is added to some wines to extend quantity. Wines that are fortified have alcohol added in the form of brandy.

In the United States, many wineries pasteurize their wine to stop all growth at the bottling stage in order to produce a uniform wine. In Europe, this is not an established practice, so there are variations in quality on a year-to-year basis. The term "vintage" means wine made from grapes of a certain year. Vintners select their best year and date the bottles. This practice has now been adopted by a number of wineries in the United States due to public demand.

There is much mystique in the production and enjoyment of wine. Each individual who drinks a glass of wine tastes something different in it, and what pleases one may not please another. Young people may enjoy modern "pop" wine, but, as their taste buds develop, they no longer like its sweetness and will sample other wines.

In selecting wine for sale, one must consider two things: first, what will the buying public demand and second, will a profit be made on it. Most customers don't want to be educated, but want to drink what they like.

Most countries produce good wine, and many produce superior ones. No one country produces the best wines. The United States has had a long history of producing good wine and in recent years has been recognized for some of its great wines. Most vineyards in the United States have converted to the *V. vinifera* variety, and the resulting quality of the wine has improved rapidly. In the remaining pages of this chapter, I have tried to list the better-known wines from around the world, including a list of wineries in the United States and their superior wines. The lists of wines are by no means complete but should offer the reader a variety to choose from.

# AMERICAN WINE

American wines today are number one in sales on the U.S. market. This has come about only since the Second World War, and the rapid increase in their acceptance is due to two factors: 1) the increasing usage of wine in the United States and 2) the vintner's concern with producing a better-quality wine.

With the switch to the *V. vinifera* grape varieties, the United States is now producing wines comparable to the imported ones. American quality control and devotion to research and experimentation will ensure an ever-increasing share of the world market. There are many small vineyards producing very fine wines, and I have tried to list the major ones with their best-known products.

## California

There are five wine-producing districts in California:

*Napa Valley:* well-balanced reds and fine whites
*Sonoma Valley:* full-bodied red wine
*Livermore Valley:* soft red wine, superior whites
*Central Valley:* sweet dark wines
*Southern Coastal:* dessert and table wines and champagne

The following is a list of California wineries and the main products of each:

*Almaden Vineyards:* Blanc de Blanc Champagne, Grenache, Rose Gewurztraminer, and Cabernet Sauvignon

*Assumption Abbey:* Assumption Abbey Angelica, Emerald Riesling, and Johannisberg Riesling

*Bealieu Vineyard:* Private Reserve, Cabernet Sauvignon, Beaumont Pinot Noir, and Chardonnay Beaufort

*Buena Vista Vineyard:* Zinfandel

*Chalone Vineyard:* Chenin Blanc and Pinot Blanc

*Chappellet Vineyard:* Chenin Blanc

*Christian Brothers:* Pineau de la Loire and Cabernet Sauvignon

*Concannon Vineyard:* Sauvignon Blanc, Cabernet Sauvignon (limited bottlings), Muscat de Frontignan, and Johannisberg Riesling

*David Bruce:* Chardonnay and Zinfandel

*Freemark Abbey Winery:* Chardonnay and Petite Sirah

*Gallo Winery:* Cabernet Sauvignon

*Hanzell Vineyard:* Chardonnay and Pinot Noir

*Heitz Wine Cellars:* Chardonnay, Cabernet Sauvignon, Angelica, and Johannisberg Riesling

*Inglenook Vineyards:* Cabernet Sauvignon (cask bottling), Pinot Noir, and Charbono

*Korbel:* Champagne, native and brut

*Hanns Kornell:* Champagne brut and Sehr Trocken

*Charles Krug:* Cabernet Sauvignon

*Llords and Elwood Winery:* Dry Sherry and Rose of Cabernet

*Louis M. Martini Vineyards:* Cabernet Sauvignon, Muscatel, and Gewurztraminer

*Paul Masson:* Champagne brut, Emerald, and Dry Riesling

*Mayacamas Vineyards:* Chardonnay and Zinfandel

*Mirassou Vineyards:* Chenin Blanc, Zinfandel, and Gewurztraminer

*Robert Mondavi Winery:* Johannisberg Riesling and Cabernet Sauvignon

*The Novitiate of Los Gatos:* Muscat Frontignan

*Oakville Vineyards:* Cabernet Sauvignon

*Martin Ray Inc.:* Blanc de Noir Champagne and Cabernet Sauvignon

*Ridge Vineyards:* Cabernet Sauvignon and Zinfandel

*Schramsberg Vineyards:* Blanc de Blanc and Blanc de Noir

*Samuel Sebastiani:* Barbera, Green Hungarian, Gewurztraminer, and Sylvaner

*Souverain Cellars Inc.:* Johannisberg Riesling

*Stony Hill Vineyard:* Chardonnay and Johannisberg Riesling

*Wente Bros.:* Pinot Blanc and Pinot Chardonnay

## New York State

The following is a list of the most distinguished wineries found in New York State, and their products.

*Boordy Vineyards:* Rose, red, and white

*Bully Hill Vineyards:* Baco Noir, Aurora Blanc, and Vineyard Red

*Gold Seal:* Pinot Noir and Johannisberg Riesling

*Great Western:* Catawba, Champagne, and Chelois

*Taylor:* Champagne, Taylor Lake Country White, Pink, and Red

*Vinifera Wine Cellars:* (Konstantin Frank) Spatlese, Riesling, Trockenbeerenauslese Riesling

*Widmer's:* Sherry, Delaware, Vergennes, Elivra Rose

## Michigan

*Bronte Champagne and Wines*

## Ohio

*Meier's Wine Cellars:* Catawba

## Washington

*Ste. Michelle Vineyards:* Semillon and Johannisberg Riesling

## FRENCH WINE

French wines are the second largest segment of the American market. For many years, they constituted the bulk of the wine sold in the world. Much of U.S. wine culture has been learned from the French, and their products are still considered the finest by connoisseurs. France has set standards that the rest of the world tries to emulate in the area of wine production. The wines are expensive, but quality excels. Much of the nomenclature of wine is French; therefore, the section on France will be the largest in this chapter.

### Districts

The three most important wine districts of France are:

1. *Gironde-Bordeaux:* clarets and white wine,
2. *Cote d'Or:* Burgundy, red, and white, and
3. *Marne:* champagne.

Additional districts are as follows:

4. *Bas Bourgogne:* Chablis,
5. *Bas-Rhin:* (Alsace),
6. *Maine et Loire:* Anjou,
7. *Indre et Loire:* Vouvray, and,
8. *Rhone:* Côtes du Rhone wines.

## The Bordeaux District

The Bordeaux district is regarded as the heart of the French wine trade. It has eight subdivisions, of which the most famous are: Medoc, Graves, Sauterne, St. Emilion, and Pomerol. The better chateaux wines from the Bordeaux district are:

Chateau Lafite-Rothschild
Chateau Latour
Chateau Olivier
Chateau Yquem
Chateau Margaux
Chateau Mouton-Rothschild
Chateau Haut-Brion

## The Cote d'Or District

The Cote d'Or district is famous for its Burgundy wines. Red Burgundy is made from Pinot grapes and white Burgundy from Pinot Blanc or Chardonnay grapes. There is no recognized chateau bottling in Cote d'Or district, but estate bottling is accepted. The six most distinct vineyards of the Cote d'Or district are as follows:

Romanee-Conti
Le Montrachet
Chambertin
Clos de Vougeot

Les Musigny
Les Bonnes Mares

The major types of wine that are produced in the Cote d'Or district are as follows:

*Maconnais, Beaujolais:* Gamay grape, clear and light; should be drunk young
*Pouilly Fuisse:* white wine
*Chablis:* dry, crisp, light, pale straw color
*Le Montrachet:* full-bodied, robust, white wine
*Sparkling Burgundy:* sweeter than champagne

## The Marne District

The Marne district is noted for the production of champagne, which is recognized as the finest in the world. According to French law, only the product made in the district of Marne can be labeled "champagne." Champagne is made from the following grape varieties (or blendings of these and other grape varieties):

Pinot Noir
Chardonnay
White Pinot

The most famous French champagne bottlers are:

Dom Perignon
Bollinger
Charles Heidsieck
Veuve Clicquot-Ponsardin
Mumm Cordon Rouge
Piper-Heidsieck
Taittinger

**The Rhone District**
The following are wines produced in the Rhone district:

> *Chateauneuf-du-Pape:* a full-bodied, red, good
> bouquet wine
> *Tavel Rose:* a well-balanced rose wine

## Labeling

French wines are strictly controlled by the government, and
the following terminology should be familiar to bartenders:

> *Chateau bottled:* bottled by the producer
> *Chateau wine:* bottled by the shipper
> *Monopole:* trademark wine
> *District or parish house label:* from a specific area

A.D.E.B. is Bordeaux wine shippers' associated seal. A
classification of growths is referred to as first, second, and
third. The first, of 1855, are considered the best of Bordeaux.
The following are labels of champagne:

> *Brut:* very dry
> *Extra sec:* dry
> *Sec:* medium sweet
> *Demi sec:* quite sweet
> *Doux:* very sweet

The following are bottle sizes for champagne:

| | |
|---|---|
| Split | 6½ ounces |
| Half bottle | 13 ounces |
| Fifth (Bottle) | 26 ounces |

| | |
|---|---|
| Magnum | 52 ounces |
| Jeroboam | 104 ounces |
| Rehoboam | 156 ounces |
| Methuselah | 208 ounces |
| Salmanazar | 312 ounces |
| Balthazar | 416 ounces |
| Nebuchadnezzar | 520 ounces |

# ITALIAN WINE

Italian wines are the third most popular in the United States, with an increasing volume imported every year. Their wines are relatively inexpensive and can compete on any market. The American public is most familiar with Chianti, a red, robust wine, but are now learning the virtue of all the different varieties that are imported. On the following pages there is a partial listing (by district) of the better Italian wines that are found on the American market.

## Piedmont District

This district is noted for its hardy wines, which travel well:

*Barbera:* a red, rough table wine

*Asti Spumante:* Moscato grape is used in its production. It is a sparkling, sweet, white wine

*Vermouth:* an aperitif wine both red and white, herb flavored, the red being the most distinguished. In the United States, vermouth is used mostly in blending of cocktails.

*Barolo:* a full-bodied, ruby-red wine

*Freisa:* a sparkling red wine, raspberry bouquet

*Cortese:* a light-bodied, straw-colored, delicate wine

*Lacrima Christi:* a dry, sparkling white wine

## Lombardy District

*Valtellina:* a light-bodied, both red and white wine
*Dr. Odero Chateau:* bottling red, rose, white, and Ambrato wines

## Venetia District

*Valpolicella:* ruby red, fine bouquet, soft
*Soave:* light, dry white wine with subtle bouquet

## Emilia District

*Lambrusco:* sparkling red wine

## Tuscany District

*Chianti:* Brolio vineyard produces an excellent, dry, red, full-bodied, rich wine
*Vin Nobile:* similar to Chianti
*White chianti* (Bianco Toscano): pleasant, full-bodied, dry white wine
*Vino dell'Elba:* fish-shaped bottle
*Vin Santo:* rich, sweet dessert wine

## Umbria District

*Verdicchio dei Castelli di Jesi:* fine, dry, light white wine
*Frascati:* fresh, dry white wine, young
*Est! Est!! Est!!!:* semi-dry, full-bouquet, golden wine

## Sicily District

*Marsala:* sweet dessert wine, golden brown to brown in color

# GERMAN WINE

Germany produces reds and sparkling wines but is most famous for its white wines. The best-known varieties are as follows:

*Liebfraumilch:* dry, white, fine wine
*Moselbluemchen (Moselle):* white wine sweeter than Rhine, a curling wine when young
*Trockenbeeren Pfalz:* sweet, clear wine
*Steinwein:* dry, white, bottled in the traditional flasklike "Bocksbeutel"
*Sekt:* sparkling white wine similar to champagne

## Labeling

To better select German wines, a bartender should be familiar with the terminology and laws governing their sales.

German wines are not blended, but each cask is bottled separately and priced accordingly. The law is very strict about the origin of wine. There are four types of labeling:

1. Estate bottled
2. Estate wine bottled by shipper
3. Parish label
4. Trade label

A list of labels follows:

*Knipperle:* labeling term, good wine, white

*Sylvaner:* labeling term, good wine, white

*Riesling:* labeling term, excellent, dry, fruity white wine

*Traminer:* labeling term, similar to Riesling

*Gewurztraminer:* spicy traminer wine of superior quality

The following bottling terms should be recognized:

*Naturwein:* natural, no sugar added

*Auslese:* selected picking

*Spatlese:* late picking

*Beerenauslese:* selected grape

*Trockenbeerenauslese:* sweetest of natural white wines

*Feine:* fine

*Wachstum:* origin of ownership

*Kellerabfullung, kellerabzug:* cellar bottling

*Schlossabzug:* estate bottled

*Bestes Fass:* best cask

*Kabinett Wein:* special reserve or selected

## SPANISH WINE

The wines of Spain were virtually unknown to the American public until after the Second World War. Most Spanish wine was produced for domestic consumption, and what little wine was exported, other than sherry, found its way to Europe. With the increasing volume of wine usage in the United States, the importation of Spanish wine has also increased. Most of the Spanish wine consumed in the United States today is not of the vintage type and is relatively low in price.

Because of the tendency of Spanish vintners to age white wine in wooden casks, Spanish white wine is yellow in color and has a slight woody flavor, which is not particularly desired by the American public. The red wines are either sweet or robust and have been well adopted on the American market.

Sherry is still the major wine; however, I have included a number of other types on the following pages.

## Sherry

*Sherry:* fortified wine made by the Solera process around Jerez. From the Palomino and Pedro Ximenez grapes, natural yeast fermentation is used
*Solera system:* blending of old wine with new to produce a standard quality

## Types of Sherry

### Finos
*Manzanilla:* fragrant, light, slightly bitter, pale in color, and very dry
*Fino:* very pale and dry with a sturdy body
*Amontillado:* fairly dry, deeper in color. An all-purpose sherry with a slightly nutty taste

### Olorosos
*Amoroso:* medium dry, golden in color. An all-purpose sherry with a nutty flavor
*Oloroso:* deep golden wine, sweet but still dry, full-bodied, heavy nutty flavor
*Cream:* very rich, dark golden, soft, sweet with full nutty flavor
*Brown:* dark brown, very sweet, full-bodied, rich nutty flavor

*Montilla:* similar to sherry from around Cordoba, not fortified. Fermented in clay pots (aged by Solera system)

## Wine Areas of Spain

Baetica, Valdepenas, Barcelona, Gerona, Valencia, Tarragona, the Balearic Islands, and Southwest Andalusia are the main wine areas of Spain.

## Types of Wine

*Wine of Rioja:* no addition of sugar, but blending with old wine sometimes occurs. Better wine that is offered will be labeled "Reserva" or "Gran Reserva," aged up to five years, including white wine. Both in casks and bottles

> *Tintos:* reds four to fifteen years old
> *Blancos:* white, woody flavor from cask again
> *Rosado:* rose
> *Sparkling wine:* similar to champagne. Softer in taste than brut, very dry

*Wine of Valdepenas:* not great or fine wine. Drunk young in three to four months. Sold in 4- or 16-litre covered glass jars. Mostly Tintos, more of a rose than a red

*Malaga:* Negro, made from Pedro Ximinez grapes, very dark

*Blanco:* golden to amber, very sweet

*Semidilace:* light in color, sweet

*Oscuro:* rich brown in color

*Amontillado:* medium dry, made from Lairen grapes

*Lagrima:* very sweet and dark

*Seco:* similar to tawny port

*Le Vente:* mostly bulk red wine with an alcoholic content of 13 to 16 percent and higher if the wine is allowed to age

*Catalonia*

*Turragona:* sweet, red, high alcoholic content

*Priorato:* red, used for blending

*Vina Corrienta:* natural white wine

*Panades:* light white wine with low alcoholic content

*Sangre de Tero:* bull's blood, ruby color, dry

*Vina Sol:* clear, dry white wine

    *Malvasia (Malmsey):* high sugar and alcoholic content

    *Sparkling wine:* made by champagne process but not called champagne, mostly white are used. Wine is very pale gold in color

*Methode Invee Close:* carbonic acid gas is added, similar to vat fermentation type in the United States.

# PORTUGUESE WINE

There are three major wine districts of Portugal:

1. Douro,
2. Estremadura, and
3. Island of Madeira.

Many good table wines are produced. However, the four most famous are: port, rose, Madeira, and muscatel. Portugal, in recent years, has been shipping chateau-bottled and table wines.

The production of port for many years has been controlled by the English.

Ports are fortified wines that normally require at least twenty years of aging for maturity.

*Vintage port:* any exceptional year is usually shipped in the cask. It normally has two dates on the label; the vintage date and the bottling date. It has the deepest ruby color and is considered to have the best body and bouquet of all ports.

*Crusted port:* not up to the standard of vintage port. It has a dark ruby color and a good fruity bouquet, usually a single vintage

*Ruby port:* a blended wine aged in wood, similar to the Solera system of Spain. Lighter in color and not as full bodied as vintage port

*Tawny:* similar to ruby port, but more pronounced woody flavor and lighter in color

*White port:* made from white grapes, considered softer than red ports

*Bucelas:* dry white wine, good bouquet, low alcoholic content

*Vino Verde:* green or young wine, rose, red, and white, bottled very young. Has a low alcoholic content, sometimes slightly sparkling. Somewhat acid but a fragrant light-bodied wine

*Rose:* slightly sparkling rose wine with carbonic acid gas added. Slightly sweet

*Muscatel:* heavy sweet wine with high alcoholic content, nut-brown color

*Madeira:* a rich fortified wine that is matured in a hothouse, brown in color and has a nutty flavor, continues to improve with age
Sercial—dry
Bual—nut brown
Malmsey—sweet

# HUNGARIAN WINE

The wines of Hungary have been famous for centuries, with Tokay being recognized as the king of wines. Hungary produces many fine wines, but unfortunately today we do not find the great estate wines of the early twentieth century. However, many good varieties of wine are imported and are well accepted.

The six wine districts of Hungary are: Alfold, Balaton, Villany-Pecs, Sopron, Eger, and Tokay. The three main types of Tokay are as follows:

*Eszencia:* rare essence of Tokay
*Aszu:* Tokay made from overripened grapes
*Szamorodni:* fresh, dry wine

Hungarian wines are further classified by the number of varieties required to produce one wine. The number can be as high as five, which is the best.

The following wines are Hungarian table wines:

*Egri Bikaver:* Bull's blood of Eger, dark garnet or red color, robust, full bodied with a spicy, pleasant aroma
*Badacsonyi Szurke-Barat:* Gray friar of Badacsony, medium-dry, golden, lively, sweet wine with a high alcoholic content
*Badacsonyi:* Blue stalks of Badacsony, very dry, vintaged, golden in color, high alcoholic content
*Debroi Harslevelu:* Linden Leaf of Drego, golden, medium-sweet, highly aromatic wine, full bodied

# CANADIAN WINE

Canadian wines do not constitute a large share of the American market. They are generally sold in the states bordering Canada and generally are similar to New York State and Ohio wines. Canada produces some very fine wines, especially from fruits such as blackberry and apple.

There are two major growing areas of Canada: the Niagara Peninsula and the Okanagan Valley of British Columbia.

The major wineries of Canada are:

*Jordan:* limited champagne
*Bright's*
*Château-Gai*
*Normandie Wines of Mauctor:* blueberry
*London Winery:* honey wines
*Andres Wines:* Rieslings, claret, and most varieties, some chateau bottled

# WINE OF OTHER NATIONS

## Argentina

Argentinian wines are highly controlled by the government, but a large amount of table wine is now being shipped to the United States, of which some is vintage quality in both red and white.

## Chile

Chile produces both table and vintage quality of German-style white wine.

## South Africa

Riesling and some good reds are produced, but a large amount is not exported to the United States.

# Israel

A sweet variety of wine is exported. There are also some Burgundy and Rhine types.

# Greece

Some Greek wines are listed here.

> *Kokkinelli:* resinated red wine.
> *Mavrodaphne:* sweet red wine from Patras.
> *Marko:* red and white table wines.
> *Tegea:* pink wine from Arcadia.

### Review and Discussion Questions

1. List the steps in the wine-making process.
2. What is the difference between a wine that is pasteurized and a vintage wine?
3. List the major color categories of wine. Give an example of each.
4. Design a wine list, using examples of the best wines from at least five countries.

# Whiskey

**Objectives**

This chapter explains the whiskey-making process. The student after studying this chapter should be able to:

1. Describe the whiskey-making process.

2. Discuss the difference between the various types of whiskeys.

3. Identify the four Scotch whiskey-making districts of Scotland.

4. Explain how whiskey receives its color and flavor.

5

Whiskey is a distilled spirit made from grains fermented and distilled at no more than 190 proof and no less than 80 proof. The word "whiskey" is Celtic in origin and means water of life. The major producing countries are the United States, Canada, Scotland, and Ireland. Other nations produce whiskey-type beverages, but very few of their products have been accepted on the American market.

## AMERICAN WHISKEY

Most whiskey produced in the United States comes from three areas, Kentucky, western Pennsylvania, and the Midwest, specifically Indiana and Illinois. The properties of the limestone spring water found in these areas are conducive to the production of fine whiskeys.

Making whiskey is a simple process, and the quality of the product is dependent on the following factors:

1. The type and quality of the grains and malt used,
2. The properties of water used,
3. The type of still (pot or twin column), and
4. The amount of aging and degree of blending.

The process of making whiskey in the United States is strictly controlled by the federal and state governments. The grains (corn, rye, barley, etc.) are ground into meal, combined with barley malt (see Chapter 3 on the making of beer), and water, and then cooked to convert the starches to sugar.

At this stage, the mixture is called "wort." The wort is cooled and transferred to fermenting tanks, and cultivated yeast is added. A sweet or sour mash process may be utilized for fermenting. The sweet mash process utilizes fresh cultivated yeast for fermentation and normally takes from 36 to 50 hours to ferment. The sour mash process uses two-thirds fresh cultivated yeast and one-third working yeast from a previous fermentation. This fermentation process takes between 72 and 96 hours. It is thought that the sour mash process produces a slightly sweeter whiskey. During fermentation, beer is produced. The beer is transferred to the still and distilled at no more than 160 proof. Water is added to reduce the proof to no more than 103 proof and no less than 100 proof. The whiskey is then transferred to new, charred white oak casks and allowed to age. During the aging process, water evaporates, thus raising the proof, and the whiskey also mellows. The whiskey changes from white to amber in color. At the time of bottling, caramel may be added to change the color even further.

The following are whiskey types made in the United States:

## Blended Whiskey

This is a blend of grain whiskeys and neutral spirits bottled at no more than 100 proof and no less than 80 proof. In most cases, this is what is used as bar whiskey for mixing drinks.

## Bourbon Whiskey

This is whiskey distilled from a fermented mash of grain that is no less than 51 percent corn grain. Both sweet and sour mash are produced. Normally, sweet mash bourbon is bar bourbon; and sour mash is dispensed when specially requested. Bourbon, originally made in Bourbon County, Kentucky, is an American product now produced in all whiskey-making areas of the United States.

## Rye Whiskey

This is a whiskey distilled from a fermented mash of grain that contains not less than 51 percent rye grain. Rye whiskey has a distinct flavor all its own and normally is sold at 100 proof. It should never be substituted for blended whiskey at the bar. It is particularly favored in the Midwest. On the East and West coasts of the United States most customers, when ordering rye and water, expect to be served a blended whiskey and not straight rye whiskey.

## Malt Whiskey

Malt whiskey is distilled from a fermented mash of grain, of which not less than 51 percent of the grain is malted barley or malted rye grain. Very little malt whiskey is produced in the United States.

## Corn Whiskey

This whiskey is distilled from a fermented mash of grain that contains not less than 80 percent corn grain. It is stored in uncharred oak casts and normally aged for only a limited period. Its color is white to pale yellow, and it has a very distinctive corn flavor. It is consumed mostly in the South and should never be substituted for any other whiskey at the bar.

## Bottled in Bond

These are whiskeys that have been distilled at not more than 160 proof, are straight whiskeys (not blended), are four years old or more, and are bottled at 100 proof. The term "bottled in bond" does not imply quality but refers to the internal revenue tax laws governing the bottling of taxable whiskeys.

# CANADIAN WHISKEY

Canadian whiskey is a distinctive product of Canada containing no distilled spirit less than two years old, and is a blended whiskey. It is produced from corn, rye, wheat, and barley malt. The method of production is similar to that of blended American whiskeys. Canadian whiskey is distilled out at 140 to 180 proof. The proof is reduced to 80 to 90 proof at bottling. Most Canadian whiskeys are aged six years; however, some of the less expensive ones are placed on the market at two years of age.

# SCOTCH WHISKEY

Scotch whiskey is only produced in Scotland. There are four major whiskey-making areas, and each produces a whiskey with its own distinctive flavor and aroma. They are:

1. Highland
2. Lowland,
3. Islay, and
4. Campbeltown.

Scotch whiskey is made from malted barley grain. There are five steps in making Scotch whiskey:

1. Malting,
2. Mashing,
3. Fermenting,
4. Distilling, and
5. Aging and Blending

The malting process should be understood, because this is what makes Scotch distinctively different from other whiskeys. Barley is steeped in water until softened and then spread out over the floors of the malting house to germinate and sprout for three weeks. The green malt is then transferred to a kiln where it is roasted over a peat fire.

During this process, the malt dries out and picks up the smoky flavor associated with Scotch whiskey. The degree of roasting is controlled, and the differences in Scotch from each separate producing area are reflected in the darkness of the roasted barley malt. For example, Campbeltown is noted for its dark roast; whereas the Lowland is sought after as a light, mild roast.

The barley malt is ground and mixed with warm water to convert the starch to sugar. The wort is transferred to a fermenting tank, and yeast is added. Beer is produced, then distilled in a pot still. It is then redistilled and proofed off at 140 to 142 proof. It is reduced to between 124 and 126.8 proof by the addition of distilled water. The whiskey produced is aged in charred white oak casks.

To create the perfect taste and aroma, the bottler blends whiskeys from all areas with grain whiskey (unmalted whiskey). This process takes place after the whiskeys are at least four years old. The fine art of making Scotch whiskey is in the hands of a blender who might use as many as fifty malt whiskeys, along with five or six grain whiskeys to attain the desired taste. A small quantity of unblended malt whiskey is sold. These whiskeys must be labeled "malt whiskey." They tend to be fuller bodied and sell at a premium. In general, the American public prefers light-bodied blended whiskeys.

Scotch that has been aged over ten years tends to be softer and mellower.

Although Scotch whiskey can only be made in Scotland, it is bottled in the United States. Some bottlers import Scotch in bulk to reduce the amount of import duty, and bottle it at the port of entry.

# IRISH WHISKEY

Irish whiskey does not command as large a market in the United States as does Scotch; however, it enjoys an excellent reputation.

Only Ireland can produce Irish whiskey. The process is similar to the production of Scotch whiskey, with the major difference being that the barley malt is not smoke cured, but heat cured with peat. A second difference is that Irish whiskey is triple distilled in pot stills. Ireland produces both blended (malt whiskey blended with grain whiskey) and single malt. Irish whiskey is aged a minimum of seven years before bottling. Irish whiskey has a less malty flavor than Scotch, and there is a growing demand for it in the United States.

Whiskey is the largest selling distilled spirit in the world. American whiskeys rank number one, with blended whiskeys being first, and Scotch second. All whiskeys have their similarities, but they are all different. The taste that pleases one customer may turn away the next. In stocking a bar, the largest section of inventory is whiskeys. Customers should always be offered a choice, and the whiskeys most called for by patrons should be carried. In mixing drinks, a premium product should be used; customers can always tell the difference.

## Review and Discussion Questions

1. What type of grain is used in the making of:
   a) Scotch whiskey, b) blended whiskey?
2. Define the terms: a) bottled in bond, b) blending.
3. Explain the difference between blended whiskey and rye whiskey.
4. What is the malting process?

# Gin

## 6

**Objectives**

This chapter explains the gin-making process and the various types of gin on the market. The student, after studying this chapter, should be able to:

1. Discuss the gin-making process.

2. Identify the major botanicals used in making gin and discuss their effect on the flavor of the finished product.

3. Identify the type of gin used in making cocktails.

4. Explain the difference in the various types of gin on the market today.

Gin is an alcoholic beverage obtained by redistilling grain spirits with flavoring agents, especially the juniper berry. Gin was first produced in Holland in the seventeenth century for medicinal purposes and was called "Genever" or "Holland." During the eighteenth century, England began producing gin, and since then its manufacture and use has spread throughout the world. Today, the production of gin is an exacting science, requiring technical experience to conform to government regulations and quality control.

## TYPES OF GIN

There are three basic types of gin: dry gin, which is light bodied and aromatic in flavor and taste; Genever, which is full flavored, with a malty aroma and taste; and the third variety, flavored gin, which has the additional flavoring of a fruit, such as orange, mint, lemon, etc. There is one additional gin called Old Tom, which is sweetened gin that is produced in England.

### Dry Gin

Dry gin, or English gin, is the most familiar type and is used for mixed drinks. It is made by mashing and fermenting a grain mixture of 75 percent corn, 15 percent barley malt, and 10 percent other grains. After the fermentation is completed, the resulting wort or beer is distilled in a patent still. The alcohol derived from the still is a 180 to 188 proof. Distilled water is then added to reduce the proof to 120. The 120 proof alcohol is then placed in a pot still with juniper berries and other botanicals and is redistilled and recovered at 170 to 180 proof. It is again reduced by the addition of distilled water and bottled at 80 to 94 proof. Gin is generally not aged, and manufacturers have their own secret formulas for the quantity and type of botanicals used for flavoring.

## Genever

The production of Genever or Dutch gin varies somewhat from dry gin. Equal parts of rye, corn, and barley malt are mashed and fermented to beer. The beer is distilled to 100 to 110 proof in a pot still, and the resulting product is called "malt wine." This is then redistilled in a pot still with juniper berries and other botanicals. The resulting gin is proofed out at 94 to 98 proof.

## Flavored Gin

In the production of fruit-flavored gins, dry gin is flavored with the oils of a specific fruit. This process is called "rectifying."

As previously stated, most gins are not aged, but a small number of distilleries produce a yellow or golden gin by the aging process. Most customers prefer dry gin, and aged gin should only be served on special request. In mixing drinks, only dry gin should be used, as Genever and flavored gins would change the flavor and characteristics of the drink.

**Review and Discussion Questions**

1. Describe the process used in the production of English dry
   gin.
2. Discuss the difference between dry gin and Genever.
3. What is the alcoholic content of: a) dry gin, b) Dutch gin?
4. What gin is preferred for making cocktails?

# Rum

## Objectives

This chapter discusses the rum-making process and the properties of each type of rum. The student, after studying this chapter, should be able to:

1. Understand the rum-making process.

2. Identify the origins and properties of the three major types of rum.

3. Explain the difference between the various types of rum and select suitable types for making bar cocktails.

7

Rum is the alcoholic distillate from the fermented juice of sugar cane, sugar cane syrup, or sugar cane molasses. It is distilled at not more than 190 proof and not less than 80 proof. Rum is actually a by-product of the sugar refinery industry.

## THE RUM-MAKING PROCESS

In the production of rum, sugar cane is crushed at the refinery, and the juice is boiled to concentrate the sugar and evaporate the water. The result will be a heavy, thick syrup. The sugar in the syrup is then crystallized and separated from the residue molasses. The low-sugar-content molasses is placed in the fermentation vat, and water is added. Yeast, whether natural or cultivated, starts the fermentation process, which takes between two and four days. The fermented mash is then distilled to 160 to 180 proof. Generally, rum is aged in oak barrels from one to four years. It is then filtered; caramel is added for coloring; and it is aged again. During the bottling process, the proof is reduced with distilled water. Some distilleries blend their new rums with older rums. Most rum is bottled at 80 proof; however, some 90, 100, and over-proof at 149 proof rums are marketed.

## TYPES OF RUM

Rum has three main classifications:

    1. Very dry, light bodied,

2. Dark, full bodied, and

3. Light bodied, aromatic.

According to the Federal Alcohol Administration, the word "type" may not be used to identify a rum; instead, the place of origin must appear on the label.

## Light-Bodied Rum

The light-bodied rums of Puerto Rico and Cuba are labeled "white" or "silver." The aged, more flavorful rums are labeled "gold" or "amber." The light-bodied rums are generally produced in the Spanish islands of the Caribbean. These rums have a very slight taste of molasses and are used in most cocktails. Virgin Island rum tends to be very light bodied and in most cases is not aged.

## Full-Bodied Rum

The full-bodied pungent rums of Jamaica, Barbados, and British Guiana (Demerara) are produced in a slightly different manner, and the resulting product is very popular for mixing specialty drinks such as Planter's Punch. The fermentation process makes the difference. The skimmings from the sugar boilers are added to the molasses and allowed to ferment naturally without the addition of cultured yeast. The fermentation process takes between five and twenty days. The pot still is utilized for the distillation process. The mash is distilled twice and run off between 140 and 160 proof. The rum is aged and blended, and at bottling the proof is reduced with distilled water to 86 proof.

Some of these rums are sold at 97, 114, and 151 proof. The 151 proof rum has limited use in a bar but is occasionally used for flaming drinks and food.

## Aromatic Rum

The third type of rum is produced in Java and is pungently aromatic. It is called Arak. Very little of it reaches the United States, but it is highly favored in the Netherlands and the Scandinavian countries. It is quite often drunk as a liqueur and is the major ingredient in Swedish Punch. The production of Arak is somewhat different from the other rums in that Javanese rice cakes are added to the mash during the natural fermentation process. Arak is aged three to four years in Java and then shipped to the Netherlands, where it is aged for an additional six years, then blended and bottled.

Full-bodied and light-bodied rums are also produced in the New England states. There are many fine rums produced throughout the world. Each distillery has its own distinctive type. Most of the rum utilized for mixing drinks in the United States is imported from Puerto Rico, Jamaica, and Barbados.

### Review and Discussion Questions

1. What are the three classifications of rum and how do they differ?
2. Identify three countries that produce rum and discuss the type each is known for.
3. Trace the rum-making process from the cane to aging.
4. Discuss proofs of the various rums on the market today.

# Vodka
# and
# Tequila

**Objectives**

This chapter discusses the properties of vodka and tequila and their production. The student, after studying the chapter, should be able to:

1. Understand the process of making vodka.

2. Explain the distillation process used in the production of tequila.

3. Discuss the proof contents of vodka and tequila and record specific types for bar service.

# 8

There are a number of other distilled spirits that are produced throughout the world, many of which are popular in the United States.

## VODKA

Vodka, originally produced in Russia, is now the number four selling distilled spirit in the world today. The dictionary defines vodka as "a colorless and unaged liquor of neutral spirits distilled from a mash (as of rye or wheat)."

Vodka may be made from any sugar-bearing plant or grain: corn, wheat, potato, or sugar beet. The patent still is utilized for the distillation process, and the resulting distillate is not aged.

Vodka, which has no distinctive flavor or aroma, is an ideal spirit to use in mixed drinks. It has the ability to pick up the flavors of fruit and other ingredients.

Vodka produced in Russia and all other Slavic countries may be flavored. The most popular type is Zubrowka, which is vodka steeped with buffalo grass. It is slightly yellow in color and has an aromatic bouquet.

## TEQUILA

Tequila is the national drink of Mexico, and a large quantity is exported throughout the world. It is made from the agave cactus plant, also known as the century plant, or mezcal.

The agave plant normally takes twelve years to grow. At

maturity, it is harvested and shipped to the distillery. At the distillery, it is split in half and steamed for twenty-four hours, and then the juice is extracted. The juice is put in a fermentation tank and allowed to ferment for two to two and one-half days. The fermented product is then distilled in a pot still. The tequila is proofed out at 104 proof. White tequila, which is most familiar to the American public, is unaged and bottled at between 80 to 100 proof. Tequila gold is aged for four years in oak casks and bottled at 100 to 110 proof for export. Very little overproof tequila is produced, and it is mainly consumed in Mexico.

If tequila is produced in a district of Mexico not adjacent to the town of Tequila, it must be labeled "mezcal." A small quantity of tequila is bottled with a ceramic worm in the bottle as a merchandising gimmick. Tequila is served in cocktails, or straight with a slice of lime and a pinch of salt.

### Review and Discussion Questions

1. Explain how vodka is made.
2. Why is vodka an ideal spirit for mixing drinks?
3. Describe how tequila is made.
4. What is the difference between mezcal and tequila, and which is exported from Mexico in the largest quantity?

# Brandy

This chapter explains the classifications of brandy and how it is processed. The student, after studying this chapter, should be able to:

1. Discuss the conversion of fruit to brandy through the process of distillation.

2. Explain the difference between cognac and brandy.

3. List the brandy-producing countries and describe what types of brandy they are best known for.

4. Explain the significance of the letter identification found on brandy bottles.

9

Brandy is obtained by the distillation of grape wine or any fermented mash of fruit. All countries that produce wine also produce brandy. The most popular brandies are from grape wine; and in the mixing of bar drinks, grape brandy is always used unless another type is specifically called for. Brandy may be flavored or plain. After the wine has been distilled, the new alcohol is placed in aging barrels to mature, smooth out, and develop color. Some distilleries add caramelized sugar for color. Most brandies are blended before bottling, and distilled water is added to reduce the alcoholic content to 80 to 100 proof.

## FRENCH BRANDY

France produces cognac from the Champagne grape, and it is matured in white oak casks. France's Armagnac is made from the Burgundy grape and is aged in black oak casks. Also, a brandy distilled from the grape pomace is made, and is called marc. France also produces brandy, not of the cognac quality, from other grape varieties. Calvados, an apple brandy, is produced with pot stills in the Normandy area.

The labeling of cognac is controlled by the French government and the ratings by quality are as follows:

1. Grande Champagne,
2. Petite Champagne,
3. Borderies,
4. Fins Bois,
5. Bons Bois,

6. Bois Ordinaires, and

7. Bois communs dits a Terroir.

The bottlers themselves rate their own brandies by stars—one, two, three, and sometimes up to five. The stars on the label do not have any significance in regard to the age of the brandy. Furthermore, letters are used to indicate quality. The letter designations are as follows:

E—Especial
F—Fine
V—Very
O—Old
S—Superior
P—Pale
X—Extra
C—Cognac

A bottler could put together any combination of the letters, for example, EFVOC, which translated means especially fine, very old cognac. Generally speaking, one is better off selecting a brandy by the reputation of the bottler and the shipper rather than by the letters on the bottle.

## AMERICAN BRANDY

Brandy production was stopped during Prohibition in the United States and is only coming back into its own in recent years. California produces the bulk of U.S. brandy. Since 1975, some very good American vintage brandy of the French type has been placed on the market.

## SPANISH BRANDY

Spain produces a good share of the world's brandy both from sherry wine and from other grape varieties. Spanish brandies tend to be sweeter than the French and United States varieties and have a distinct flavor, especially those derived from sherry wine. Brandies are blended by the Solera system to generate a uniform product. The outstanding shippers generally are those involved in the sherry trade.

## ITALIAN BRANDY

Italy produces both brandy and its own cognac. Italian cognac is quite sweet and is not recommended for use in mixed drinks in American bars. Italy also produces a product called grappa, similar to French marc, which is colorless and quite raw.

## PORTUGUESE BRANDY

Portugal produces brandies from both port wines and other grape varieties. Portuguese brandy is relatively sweet, and a small quantity is exported to the United States.

## PERUVIAN BRANDY

Peru produces a brandy type named Pisco from the muscat grape. It is aged in clay jars and sold when it is fairly young. It is used in the United States primarily for Pisco Sours.

## GREEK BRANDY

There is a great deal of brandy distilled in Greece, and it is becoming increasingly popular. It has a clean, sweet flavor. The most popular Greek brandy sold in the United States is Metaxa. The distinctive ouzo, flavored with anise and licorice, is a colorless brandy, but when mixed with water it turns milky.

# ISRAELI BRANDY

Israel produces a small amount of grape brandy that is quite sweet and is kosher.

# FRUIT BRANDY

Other fruits are used throughout the world to make brandy; each has its own qualities and characteristics. In the United States, apple jack, from the apple, competes with the French calvados. Cherry, blackberry, prune, and apricot are some of the most appreciated fruit brandies. In purchasing fruit brandies, one should make sure to buy a true fruit brandy and not a fruit-flavored one. Fruit-flavored brandy may be made from any brandy and is flavored with the essence of the fruit by either the infusion or percolation process. A brandy is generally served after dinner, straight, or mixed in a cocktail.

### Review and Discussion Questions

1. Explain the difference between cognac, Armagnac, and calvados.
2. How is French brandy classified?
3. Explain the difference between fruit brandies and fruit-flavored brandies.

# Liqueurs
# and
# Cordials

## Objectives

This chapter discusses liqueurs
and cordials, with emphasis on
methods of production and classification. The student, after
studying this chapter, should be
able to:

1. Discuss the two major classifications
   of liqueurs and give examples of
   each.

2. Explain the three methods of liqueur production.

3. Identify the nationality and flavor of the major
   cordials on the market today.

# 10

A liqueur is an alcoholic beverage made by combining a spirit with flavorings, then adding sugar syrup in excess of 2.5 percent of the volume. The term "cordial" is synonymous with liqueur. There are two major types of liqueurs: those that are fruit based and natural colored, and those that are plant or botanically flavored.

For many years, cordials were sold as medicine or love potions. Today, in most cases, they are served as after-dinner drinks or mixed with other ingredients to make cocktails.

The alcoholic spirit that the flavoring is combined with is, in most cases, grape brandy. However, the less expensive liqueurs may use neutral spirits. There are three basic methods of flavoring the alcoholic spirits. They are:

1. Distillation,
2. Percolation, and
3. Infusion.

## DISTILLATION

The distillation method is similar to the process of making gin. The flavoring agents (botanicals) are soaked in brandy overnight. The mildly flavored spirit and the herbs are then placed in a pot still and redistilled. The distillate derived from this process is a colorless, flavored spirit. The producer then adds sugar, in the amount of not less than 2.5 percent by volume, to achieve the degree of sweetness desired. Vegetable coloring is then added to produce the color. Thus, it is possible to have brown or white creme de curacao and even blue creme de menthe. Many of the plant liqueurs are aged in wooden casks to mature and achieve full flavor.

## PERCOLATION

The percolation method is also utilized in the production of plant liqueurs. It is similar to the process of brewing coffee. Brandy or neutral spirits are constantly pumped over the flavoring agent and allowed to percolate through it, soaking up the natural flavor of the botanical. The resulting flavored spirit is then filtered, with sugar syrup and vegetable coloring added for sweetness and color. The liqueur can either be bottled immediately or aged in wooden casks.

## INFUSION

The third method of production (infusion) is used primarily in the making of fruit liqueurs. Brandy or neutral spirits are put in a vat with fresh or dried fruit and allowed to steep for up to a year. The liquid is drained off, the residue fruit distilled, and the resulting distillate added to the fruit brandy. Sugar syrup is added, and the product is aged from six months to a year. Many different fruits are used, but the most popular are apricot, cherry, peach, and blackberry.

Cordials are produced all over the world and by many different companies. The better varieties use brandy, not natural spirits, with true fruit and botanicals, not essences. Each producer has his or her own secret and unique formula, some of which have never been duplicated. Alcoholic content varies by company.

In selecting liqueurs for a bar, thought should be given to what ones are required for popular mixed drinks, and which varieties are demanded by customers. On the following pages is a list of popular liqueurs. The list is by no means complete.

# LIQUEURS AND CORDIALS TERMINOLOGY

*Anisette:* licorice flavored, the Italian (Anesone) is 90 proof, Spanish (Anis) is 78 to 96, United States produces 50 proof, Ojen (Spanish) is 84 to 100 proof, ouzo (Greek) is 98 proof

*Apricot:* (Apry) apricot flavored, 60 to 70 proof

*Benedictine:* plant liqueur made by the Benedictine monks of France, with a base of fine cognac brandy, 86 proof

*B & B:* (Benedictine and brandy) fine French brandy added to Benedictine to make a drier beverage, 86 proof

*Blackberry:* 60 to 70 proof

*Chartreuse:* plant liqueur made by the Carthusian Fathers. Yellow, 86 proof, and green, 110 proof, made in France

*Cherry liqueur:* (Cherry Heering, Danish) usually obtained from wild cherries, 49 to 70 proof

*Creme d'ananas:* pineapple flavored, 60 proof

*Creme de bananes:* banana flavored, 60 proof. Note: Unlike most fruits, the banana will not render its flavor; therefore, manmade banana flavoring must be added

*Creme de cacao:* (brown and white) made from cacao and vanilla beans, 50 to 60 proof

*Creme de cassis:* (French) made from black currants, 36 to 50 proof

*Creme de fraises:* strawberry liqueur, 40 to 60 proof

*Creme de framboises:* raspberry, 60 proof

*Creme de menthe:* (green, white, pink, etc.) either peppermint or spearmint, 54 to 60 proof. The peppermint is preferred for mixed drinks.

*Creme de noyaux:* (bitter almond flavor) made from fruit pits, 60 proof

*Creme de rose:* rose flavored, made from the oil of rose petals and vanilla, 60 proof

*Creme de vanilla:* made from the Mexican vanilla bean, 60 proof

*Curacao:* made from the dried peel of green orange from the island of Curacao, 54 to 60 proof. Note: Triple Sec is a white curacao at 60 proof.

*Drambuie:* Scotch liqueur made from malt Scotch whiskey and heather honey, 80 proof

*Galliano:* aromatic plant liqueur from Italy, 78 proof

*Goldwasser:* (gold water) orange and herb flavored with flecks of gold leaf, 80 proof

*Grand Marnier:* a type of curacao made in France with fine cognac, 80 proof

*Kahlua:* coffee liqueur from Mexico, 53 proof

*Kummel:* caraway, 86 proof

*Maraschino:* made from the Dalmatian marasca cherry, 64 proof

*Mastikha:* (Greek) made from the gum of the mastikha plant, 90 proof

*Parfait Amour:* Plant liqueur from violet and other flowers, lilac in color, 60 proof

*Peach liqueur:* made from fresh and dried peaches

*Peppermint schnapps:* similar to creme de menthe; however, has less peppermint flavoring and sweetening, 60 proof

*Prunelle:* made from plums, 50 to 60 proof

*Rock and Rye:* rye whiskey with a syrup of rock candy, sometimes with a rock candy crystal in the bottle, 70 proof

*Sloe gin:* made from the sloe berry (not a gin), 60 proof

*Southern Comfort:* bourbon whiskey with rock candy crystals, 100 proof

*Strega:* spicy plant liqueur from Italy, 80 proof

*Tia Maria:* Coffee liqueur from Jamaica, 63 proof

## Review and Discussion Questions

1. Discuss the two types of flavoring agent used in making cordials.
2. Explain the three processes that may be used in producing liqueurs.
3. Discuss the use of cordials in the American bar.
4. Write up a beverage list of cordials a bartender might encounter in a bar lounge.

# Bar Setup

## Objectives

In this chapter, the student will encounter a description of the physical layout of the four major types of bars and a discussion of the problems with each. The student, after studying this chapter, should be able to:

1. Discuss the layout and operation of the four major bar types.

2. Explain the service problems encountered in a lounge operation.

3. List the major pieces of bar equipment found in a small bar operation.

4. Discuss bar setup, including the listing of bar implements needed to operate the bar.

**11**

There are four basic types of bar operations. They are:

1. Stand-up,
2. Service,
3. Cocktail lounge, and
4. Catering.

Each one has its own distinctive operating problems, but all are similar in some ways.

## THE STAND-UP BAR

The stand-up bar is the operation Americans are most familiar with. It is misnamed, because today most customers do not stand up at the bar, but sit on stools. Due to the high turnover of customers during busy periods, this is the most exacting station for a bartender. The working space is confined, and the bartender is constantly in front of the public. The bartender not only has to be accurate in mixing drinks and cashing, but also must be somewhat of a showman in displaying skill to the ever-present audience. Due to the limited amount of working space behind the bar, the bartender must at all times be neat and orderly. The bartender is in personal contact with customers at all times and therefore must have a friendly, engaging personality and the ability to get along with the public.

At the stand-up bar, the bartender becomes aware very quickly of the regular customers' preferences in brands, and the changes in fad drinks. One of his responsibilities is to inform management of these preferences and changes, so that the bar may be adequately stocked. The location of the bar, as to the area of the country and the type of clientele, will influence the types of drinks in most demand. Hotel stand-up bars will sell less beer and wine and more mixed drinks, compared to neighborhood bars.

The bartender, in most cases, is on his own. He must not only be responsible for the dispensing of drinks, cashiering, and normal operations, but also must control the bar and its patrons.

## Straight-Line Bar with Closed Ends

There are many designs for bars, but basically there are three categories. The largest number would fall under the category of straight line with closed ends. This type of bar can project into the room or be recessed. The advantage of this type is that the bartender never has to turn his or her back to the customer and is always in control of the room. There is no regulation as to size; however, many industry people believe that one bartender to a maximum of every ten lineal feet in a high-speed bar is most efficient in service. When the bar is longer, it has multiple stations, with bartenders sharing some equipment and supplies. During slack periods, when one bartender is on duty, he or she covers the other stations.

## The Horseshoe Bar

The U-shaped, or horseshoe, bar is usually designed with three or more stations, projecting into the room, with the back end abutting a room wall. Rather than having a back bar, there is an island in the center which is used for storage and refrigeration.

## The Circular or Hollow Square Bar

The third major category is the circular or hollow square bar. It is free standing, with an island center for storage. There are few advantages to this type of bar and many disadvantages. It can be spectacular as the focal point in lounge decor; however, it is difficult to service and stock. During slow periods, the bartender on duty must try to control and service four separate areas, some of which cannot be kept in view at all times.

# THE SERVICE BAR

The service bar is found in hotels or large restaurants. It is a behind-the-scenes operation, and there is no contact between the customer and the bartender. It is generally used to service dining room patrons, with waitresses or waiters placing the orders at the service bar and serving the guests.

The service bar sells a larger quantity of wine than any other bar, and the bartender must be more familiar with its storage and care. Most service bars tend to carry a much smaller inventory than a front-of-the-house bar, and the bartender makes a much smaller variety of mixed drinks. The bartender must be able to get along with fellow restaurant employees and work with speed. The service bar is generally a straight line bar: compact, but set up similarly to the front bar. It is usually small, confining, and in many cases located in a hot, unpleasant area. This is the least desired station for a bartender because of the working conditions and the lack of tips. Therefore, it is usually assigned to a new bartender.

In the hotel or restaurant where there is a central cashiering or checking system, the service bartender will not have a bank nor be responsible for the handling of the cash. The waiter or waitress takes the guest order on a guest check and hands the check to the service bartender for filling. When the bartender completes the order, the waiter/waitress serves it and has the cashier price it out. If it is a high-speed service bar, the waitress or waiter is responsible for garnishing the drinks. In better-quality establishments, mixed drinks are placed in small glass decanters and poured into the cocktail glasses at the table.

If the bartender is in charge of the dining room wine, he or she should have access to refrigerators and a storage area for red wines. The ideal wine storage temperature for red wine is 58°F (15°C), which will not be found in a production kitchen. In many cases, red wines will be racked and displayed in the air-conditioned dining room under the control of the cashier or headwaiter.

## THE COCKTAIL LOUNGE

The cocktail lounge is the most prized job for a bartender. The pace is slower, customers generally stay for a longer period of time, and in many cases there is music or some form of entertainment. The bar is more spacious and generally accommodates more than one bartender. Physically, the bar is larger and broken down into two or more stations, with a bartender responsible for each station.

There is a service station where cocktail waiters/waitresses pick up drink orders for lounge customers, and its operation is similar to the service bar in the kitchen. Guest checks should be used for both the lounge area and the stand-up bar area. The waitresses/waiters are responsible for the collection of their own checks and in many cases have their own banks.

In the case of a large-volume cocktail lounge, there is a cashier to handle the money, and a bar boy or girl will be assigned the task of cleaning, washing glassware, and replenishing supplies. There may also be a room manager in charge of the complete operation.

It is not standard policy, but in some cases there is a pooling of tips. This eliminates much friction between the bartender and the cocktail waitress.

The same basic designs found in the stand-up bar are found in the cocktail lounge, with the addition of table and booth seating. Aisles must be adequate so that guests and waiters may get to all areas of the lounge. Space must be allotted for entertainment, and, where needed, a dance floor must be provided.

## THE CATERING BAR

Catering bars are found in hotels, catering houses, and large restaurants. They can be either portable or in a fixed place. The bar is open only for a specific group of people for a set period of time and can be operated on a cash-per-drink basis or paid for with a single check. Experienced bartenders prefer working a catering bar because of the short hours and the opportunity of making a high salary in tips.

It takes an experienced bartender to operate a catering bar. He or she must be a high-speed, organized worker. The bartender must set up the bar completely prior to opening it and be responsible for stocking it with beverages, equipment, glassware, ice, and all supplies needed to operate it. After the function is completed, the bartender must inventory the remaining stock, cash out, or, in the case of a single check bar, make out the guest check. The bartender is also responsible for cleaning the bar and securing the beverage inventory either by locking it in a cabinet or returning it to the beverage stock room.

There are a number of types of catering operations, and a bartender should be familiar with each. The limited-service bar serves highballs, a limited variety of premixed cocktails, (Martini, Manhattan, Whiskey Sour, and Daiquiri), and beer. The full-service bar offers a large variety of choices but a limited variety of brands.

If it is a cash bar, all drinks are generally sold at a fixed price: for example, all mixed drinks are $1.50, beer $1.00, and soft beverages $.50. This is done to speed up service and alleviate confusion in cashiering. The single-check catering bar is much easier for the bartender, in that he or she does not have to collect payment for every drink. He or she takes a beginning inventory of beverages before opening and then takes an ending inventory at closing, and the difference is the amount of beverages sold. The individual or company that has contracted for the party is billed either on a per-bottle fixed charge or on a per-drink basis.

The catering bar is generally of the straight-line design and set up for efficiency and speed. The same rule applies for size, in that there is one bartender for every ten lineal feet. However, many catering managers feel that a catering bartender should be able to handle one hundred persons per hour during a cocktail party.

## BARS AND BARTENDING

Bars are designed for efficiency and service. Two things must be kept in mind: 1) they must be attractive and appealing to the guests, and 2) they must also return a profit to the owners. Controls should be built in for the protection of the guest, the owner, and the employee.

Whatever type of bar the bartender is assigned to, he or she must be professional in work and attitude. Tips are an attracting aspect but should not influence the handling of individual guests.

## PHYSICAL MAKEUP OF BARS

The physical makeup of all bars are similar and are broken down into two separate areas, the front and back bar. The front is the working area, with the actual bar and its underneath working surface. The top of the bar is used to serve guests and give them a place to set their drinks. The under bar is the bartender's work area and must be designed for maximum efficiency and sanitary control. The modern under-bar work area is made of stainless steel, and has a three-compartment sink with drain boards. It has a well, or speed rack, for storage of bar liquor bottles, ice bin, and glass storage area. It has a dispensing unit for mixes and, if draught beer is served, a dispenser unit for it.

The back bar is a storage unit. The top serves as storage area for liquor bottles, glasses, and the cash register. The unit itself may be refrigerated for the storage of beer and white wines. It also has a locked cabinet for dry storage of red wines and extra bar inventory and paper supplies. In many cases, an ice machine is also included in the unit.

The aisle between the front and back bar should be no smaller than three feet wide, with no obstruction projecting into it. Duck boards or rubber matting should be on the floor for the bartender's safety.

The term "wet bar" applies to a bar that has sewer and water lines hooked up to the front bar. Portable bars in most cases would be classified as "dry sink bars" and no washing of glasses would be done at them. Portable bars also do not generally have a full back bar but just a storage surface for glasses and bottles.

On the following pages are lists of bar supplies and equipment with which bartenders should be familiar.

## BAR IMPLEMENTS

Cocktail shakers and mixing glasses
Cutting board
Knife (fruit)
Knife (fruit peeler)
Juice squeezer

Corkscrew
Bottle opener
Can opener
Strainers for cocktail shaker
Stirring spoon
Swizzler
Ice pick
Ice tongs
Ice scoops
Muddler (a wooden implement for crushing sugar
cubes or fruit)
Shot glass
Salt shakers (salt, nutmeg, pepper)
Sugar (bar and cubes)
Bar napkins
Tooth picks
Bar towels
Antibacterial agent
Glass soap
Electric blender
Water pitcher

## GARNISHES

Olives (green)
Cocktail onions
Cocktail cherries
Lemons
Oranges
Limes
Celery stalks

# MIXES

Club soda
Ginger ale
Cola
7-Up
Tonic
Rose's Lime Juice
Worcestershire sauce
Hot sauce
Bitters
Milk
Heavy cream
Tomato juice
Orange juice
Lime juice
Lemon juice
Simple syrup

# GLASSWARE

Beer shell (8 to 10 oz.)
Cocktail (4½ oz.)
All-purpose wine (8 oz.)
Brandy snifter (5 oz.)
Pony (1 oz.)
Sherry (4 oz.)
Whiskey Sour (5 oz.)
Old Fashioned (6 oz.)
Highball (8 oz.)
Collins (12 oz.)
Rocks (8 oz.)

# BAR EQUIPMENT

*Front bar to include:*
Well for bar liquor (or speed rack)
Three-compartment sink with drain boards
Swing-out garnish tray
Draught beer dispenser unit
Soft drink dispenser unit
Empty bottle racks
Refuse container
Upper bar and lower work surface

*Back bar to include:*
Cash register
Locked storage for unopened bottles
Display area for call beverages
Wine and beer coolers
Refrigerated unit for storage of garnishes and mixes
Ice machine
Glass storage

## Review and Discussion Questions

1. Describe the four types of bar operations.
2. Discuss the problems that might be encountered in a service bar.
3. Explain differences between the stand-up bar operation and a cocktail lounge.
4. List the necessary bar implements found in a service bar.

# The Bartender
# as an Industry
# Professional

It is the objective of this chapter to introduce the student to the bartender's duties. The student after studying this chapter should be able to:

1. Identify the personality traits and the training needed to be a professional bartender.

2. Discuss the bartender's job in relation to preparation, service, control, and closing duties.

3. Differentiate between the shaking and stirring processes for mixing cocktails.

4. Design a beverage control system for a bar operation.

**12**

Mixology is the art of mixing. This does not define mixologists or bartenders' personalities. Bartenders can be compared to chefs or chemists who follow a recipe or formula to produce a product to specifications. They are managements' representatives, and must serve guests in a manner that reflects the hospitality and atmosphere of the establishments in which they work. To be good mixologists, or bartenders, they have to do a great deal more than mix drinks.

Essentially, bartenders deal with people who desire to be entertained or to escape from the pressures of their normal lives. The bar is the bartenders' normal surroundings because it is their place of work; but for guests it is a haven away from the constant turmoil of today's society.

Bartenders must be highly skilled individuals with pride in their work, a desire to please, and the ability to get along with other people. They must be neat in appearance and tidy in their habits. Many bartenders start off as bar assistants and learn their trade by watching experienced bartenders, or by attending a bartender school. Bartenders must have knowledge of their product, the customers' needs, and managements' objectives.

The bartender's job can be broken down into the following areas:

1. Preparation,
2. Service,
3. Control, and
4. Closing.

# PREPARATION

Upon reporting to their shifts, bartenders have a number of responsibilities before they can actually mix drinks. This is the preparation segment of the job, and enough time should be allotted for it so the bartender is adequately prepared to serve customers. The bartender checklist (see Chapter 11) may be compared to the pilot's flight check. It is a routine that is followed automatically to ensure that all the necessary supplies are there and that equipment is in order.

## Personal Appearance

Bartenders reporting for work must be neat in appearance, freshly shaved, hair combed, bathed, and attired in a clean uniform. In the club or hotel bar, bartenders wear white shirts, black ties, tux pants, and uniform coats. Uniforms vary for each establishment, but they should be worn with dignity.

## Bar Sanitation

Upon entering the bar, the bartender should check the lighting and temperature of the room. The bar itself must be clean and free from odor, the sink must be filled with fresh water, soap, and antibacterial agent, bar towels must be replenished, and the glasses should be clean and sparkling.

## Stocking Bar

Liquors should be brought up to par stock, and the well liquors should be placed in their racks. Coolers should be checked and restocked with wine and beers. Pressure of the draught beer unit and mixes must be regulated and checked for content. Dry store items (for example, nonchilled wines, paper goods, and linens) should be replenished. Ice for the bar should be at capacity.

## Garnishes and Juices

In most bars, garnishes are prepared before the actual opening of the bar. Cherries and olives are opened; oranges, lemons, and limes are sliced; and lemons are peeled for twists. Any additional fruit that might be used, such as mint for juleps, should be made ready. Fruit juices (orange, lemon, and tomato) should be prepared. If simple syrup is used at the bar, sufficient quantity for the shift should be prepared. In states that allow premixing of drinks, many high-volume bars premix Martinis, Manhattans, and Whiskey Sours at this time.

## Bartender's Bank

Before opening the bar, if it is a cash bar, the bartender is issued a bank in sufficient quantity to handle his or her needs during that shift. It is the bartender's daily responsibility to count the bank and replenish the change from the main cashiers. The cash register should be cleared and the tape checked. If the bar is using guest checks for dining rooms or lounge service, the bartender should obtain a sufficient supply from the accounting office and check their numerical sequence. In many hotels and restaurants, management places a dollar value on each check, and if any are lost the bartender is held responsible.

## SERVICE

Once the bartender has finished the checklist, he or she can begin work, which is Part 2 (service at the bar).

An experienced bartender has memorized the proper recipes for the drinks most often served. When a customer orders a mixed drink unknown to the bartender, the bartender should refer to a bartender's guide (many bars use *Mr. Boston,* or a similar one). Recipes should be followed precisely, measured accurately, and garnished properly.

There are three basic types of mixed drinks:

1. Those made in the glasses in which they are served,
2. Shake drinks, and
3. Stirred drinks.

The latter two will be made in the bar shaker glass.

## Drinks Made in Glasses

Highballs, Old Fashioneds, and Collinses are examples of the first group. In making this type of drink, a clean sparkling glass is selected, and cubed ice is placed in the glass. It should be noted that the bartender never uses the glass for scooping up the ice out of the ice machine, and the glass should never be more than three quarters full of ice. The desired alcohol is accurately measured and added to the iced glass, and the mix is placed in the glass last. Before being served to the guest, it must be stirred and garnished.

## Shake Drinks

Shake drinks are shaken for three reasons: first, to blend the ingredients; second, to chill them; and third, to increase the liquid volume of the finished product. In making the shake drink, ice is placed in the shaker, liquor is added, and the other ingredients are placed in the shaker last (carbonated beverages are never shaken). The top is placed securely on the shaker, and it is shaken vigorously. To serve the drink, the top of the shaker is removed and the drink is strained into the cocktail glass. The drink is then garnished and presented to the customer. If the customer has requested that the drink be served "on the rocks," a rock glass is used instead of the customary cocktail glass, and fresh ice is placed in it before straining the cocktail into it. The customary garnish would still be used.

## Stirred Drinks

The process for making stirred drinks is exactly the same as for shaken drinks, except that they are stirred rather than shaken. The reason for stirring cocktails is similar to that for shaking; however, most stirred drinks have wine as an ingredient and the shaking process would bruise the wine, which would change the appearance and flavor of the drink.

As mentioned previously, the volume of liquid is increased by shaking and stirring. While shaking a cocktail, bartenders use cubed ice which melts at a rate of ½ to ¾ ounce per 10 seconds of shaking. Stirred drinks should be made with cracked ice which melts at the same rate as ice in shaken drinks. Cocktails that utilize an egg as one of their ingredients expand up to 2.5 ounces during the shaking process. Shaved ice is used for making frappes. When a frozen drink is called for (for example, a Frozen Daiquiri), an electric blender is used instead of the shaker.

The cocktail is an American drink and there are as many varieties as there are people to invent them. The individual tastes of guests determine the types the bartender serves. The important thing is to have standards, but be flexible enough to try and please individual customers. Quality ingredients ensure a quality drink only when the bartender follows a recipe accurately. Many potentially superb drinks are ruined by the use of poor-quality mixes.

There are many juices and juice substitutes on the

market, and they should be chosen with caution. If the bar is a quality one, catering to the money market, consideration should be given to fresh squeezed orange, lemon, and lime juice. The frozen juices that are available on the market today are an excellent substitute, and many of the dehydrated products are acceptable. Some bars will add a foamy agent to shake drinks, which smooths out the flavor. This is an acceptable practice and in many cases will make the drink more palatable to customers.

One further note about shaking drinks is that the shaker must be perfectly clean for each new preparation. Drinks that are made with a milk, cream, or egg base leave a residue on the shaker glass which is hard to remove, and it will ruin any other drink if allowed to remain on the shaker glass.

The two types of liquor used at the bar are *call liquor* (those liquors ordered by brand name) and *bar* or *well liquor*, which is utilized for mixing the average drink. Management generally has a policy that if a customer orders a drink and requests a specific brand there will be an upward adjustment in price for the drink, as compared to the set price for drinks made from bar liquor.

## CONTROL

Phase three of the bartender's job is the control process. Accounting for beverage sales is one of the bartender's functions that unfortunately does not receive much time during the training period. Accounting is left to the accountant, and it is assumed that cashiering can be learned very rapidly. Why waste the bartender's time, when he or she should be learning to mix drinks? The answer is very simple: Without controls there would be no profit, and the bartender would be doing only a part of his or her job. Controlling the flow of alcoholic beverages and the cash at the bar is not only necessary but mandatory.

## Beverage Flow

Control means regulating and accounting for the flow of beverage and monies. Obviously, the bartender's first responsibility is controlling the beverage flow. There are three basic systems:

1. The measured shot glass,
2. Metered bottles, and
3. The electronic dispensing system.

### The Manual System of Measured Drinks

The manual system of measured drinks (using a shot glass) is the most accurate and costs very little to put into operation. Its major advantage is that customers accept it. Experienced bartenders fight the system, saying it slows down the operation and that they can be just as accurate when free pouring. Nothing can be further from the truth. A well-trained bartender can be just as fast with a shot glass as in free pouring. Without an accurately measured drink, the customer and the owner are both being cheated. No two drinks will ever be the same, and the number of drinks obtained from a bottle will vary with each bartender unless they are properly measured.

### The Metered Bottle System

The metered bottle system was introduced a number of years ago to fill the control gap that is inherent in the shot glass system. Locked meters are placed on the individual bottles in the store room, and then the bottle is issued to the bar. Each time a drink is poured from the bottle it measures out an exact amount of beverage, and the meter records it. The meter can be preset to measure any amount the owner desires to be utilized in the bar. At the beginning of a bartender's shift, all meters are read, and at the end of a shift they are also read. The difference between the two is the amount of beverage used during the shift. A direct ratio can be established between the two: this is the amount of beverage used during the shift. A direct ratio can be established between the amount of cash receipts on the cash register and the amount of beverage dispensed by meter readings.

It is an excellent control system, but it also has its disadvantages. Customer acceptance, for some unexplained reason, has been poor; and bartenders feel that it is too time consuming because the metered bottles pour slower than the ones without meters. The other major objection by bartenders is that if they need 1½ oz. for a specific drink, and the meters are preset at 1 oz., they have problems in accounting for the other ½ oz. Management also has a justified objection, in that the meters are expensive and they have to tie up a great deal of capital in inventory of equipment. If control is a paramount problem, then the expense of the system is justified since it can reduce loss.

### The Electronic Dispensing System

The third, and newest, system is the electronic dispensing system which may be tied into the cash register or may be self-contained with its own microcomputer or data processing system. It is only recommended for high-volume bars that need a sophisticated control system. Surprisingly enough, most bartenders accept it and may prefer it to any other system. It speeds up service, produces accurately measured drinks, and takes much less work on the bartender's part. The biggest resistance to the system is from the customer, and justifiably so, as the human element and pride have been taken out of the process. The disadvantage in the system, other than the cost, is that not all of the inventory of call beverages can be placed in the system. Therefore, only selected fast-selling liquor is controlled, and another type of control system must be utilized for the other items in stock. The photos on the following pages illustrate typical dispensing and cashiering systems.

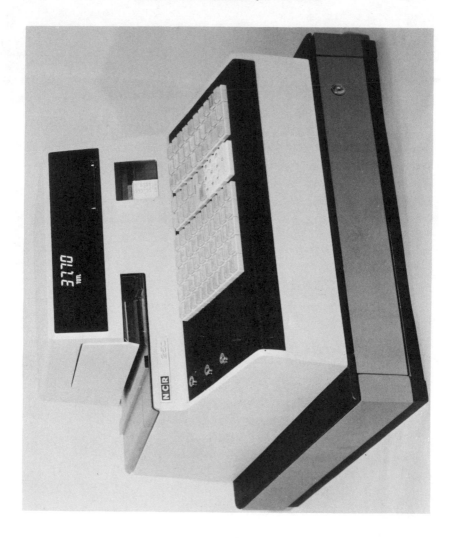

**ABOVE:** NCR cash register utilized in a pre-check control system. This model enables the operator to have a per shift check on all phases of the operation and it also may be utilized for inventory control.

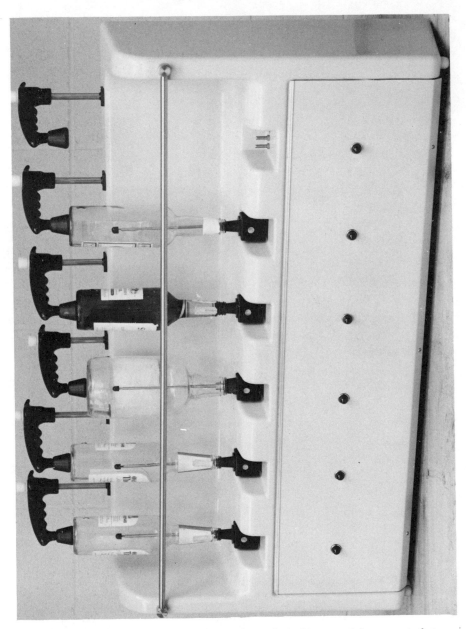

**ABOVE:** Storage unit for the post-mix system. One advantage of the system is that the storage unit may be remote, which provides locked security. A second advantage of the system is that all alcohol dispensed is measured accurately, thus, a better control is maintained. **OPPOSITE:** This is an example of a modern bartender's station equipped with liquor in Speed Racks and a post-mix dispensing system for high-volume beverage operation.

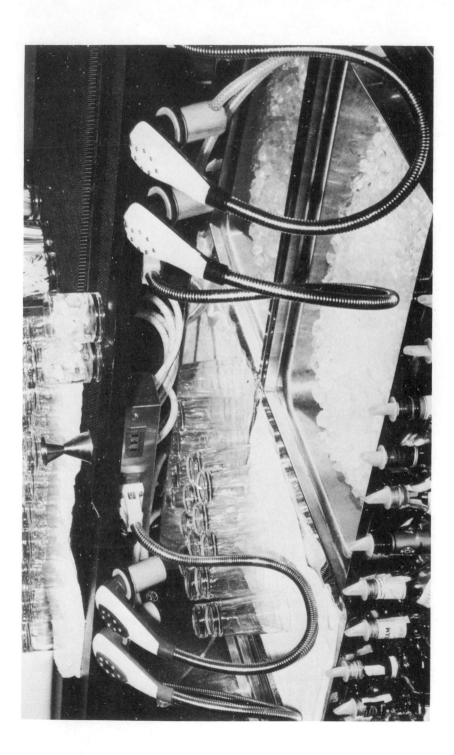

**ABOVE:** This is an example of the post-mix dispenser head and flex-hose connection system. For speed and accurately measured drinks, this unit is utilized in a high-traffic bar. **OPPOSITE:** The portable bar pictured is equipped with a post-mix system. The advantage of the unit is the compactness of the bar and the controls that are built into the unit. The bar may be utilized in any function room, and management can maintain an excellent beverage control system for the function.

## The Cashiering Process

The second area of control is the cashiering process. There are many systems, from the simplest cash box to the electronic register. Obviously, the cash box offers little or no control, and is merely a storage container for monies. The cash register may be a simple one that merely stores money, or a highly sophisticated one that furnishes a detailed sales analysis at any given time. A reasonably priced machine should have the ability to print on a running tape each transaction, with a subtotal and total key. It may also produce a guest receipt for the customer. If it is used at a multiple-station bar, it should have more than one cash drawer, with individual identification keys for each bartender. Another type of register is the precheck machine that prints on a prenumbered guest check. For lounge operation, this type of machine is a must. The cocktail waitress fills out her own check. The bartender makes the drinks and prices them on the machine, thus recording the transaction. The cocktail waitress has the responsibility of collecting from the guest and paying the bartender.

The newest development in cash registers is the electronic register. It is the most costly of all systems but is capable of performing many functions. If it is used in conjunction with the electronic dispensary system, it is the ideal control. The combination unit can have a precheck capability, and before dispensing commences, the drink must be run up. The electronic register can offer the following added control features:

1. Information storage for inventory control,
2. Detailed sales analysis with automatic price lookup,
3. Automatic tax calculations, and
4. Capability of automatic price change for special promotion of "happy hour" periods.

Any control is only as good as management's enforcement of it. Basically, bartenders are honest employees and are only made dishonest by temptation or disinterested management. Any control system may be bypassed. If any of the following list of practices is observed in a bar operation, it is indicative of poor management and the possibility of loss through theft.

1. Bartender works with an open cash drawer,
2. Bartender underpouring (short alcohol drinks),
3. Hydrometer test of bottled spirit shows less than required alcoholic proof of contents,
4. Bartender brings in own liquor,
5. Bartender or cocktail waitress/waiter brings in own guest checks,
6. Missing guest check,
7. Frequent erasure on guest check,
8. Employees shortchanging guest,
9. Frequent overcharging of guest,
10. Check padding (adding drinks to the bill),
11. Employees drinking on the job, and
12. Collusion between bartender and cocktail waitress/waiter.

## Management and the Bartender

Management also exerts control by setting policy as to the bartender's conduct and responsibility for handling customers. Basically, the bartender has to maintain discipline on the premises, and this can only be accomplished with the right attitude. Bartenders should be friendly, but not familiar, never drink on duty, nor favor one guest over another, and should remember at all times that the bar is run for two purposes:     1) profit for the owners, and 2) convenience of the guests.

Many bartenders feel it is their bar and they have the right to set policy. Nothing could be further from the truth. Ownership has an investment, and the bar's reputation is made from their direction and policies.

Many bartenders feel it is their right to give good customers a free drink after several paid rounds, or pour free drinks for fellow employees or an occasional drink for themselves or friends. All drinks must be accounted for, and if any are to be given away, it should be at the owner's discretion, not the employees'.

When there is a television or radio in the bar, it is for the guests' entertainment. Choice of channels and type of music should be for the customers' convenience and not the employees'.

## Controlling the Bar

Bartenders must know the technical aspects of the trade, but even more importantly, they must serve guests in a manner that creates an atmosphere of cordiality. They also must show restraint when dealing with the public. They must have the ability to say "no" when customers want more drinks than they have the ability to pay for or handle. Bartenders must be aware of all laws governing the sale of alcoholic beverages, especially those dealing with minors. They must know how to handle drunken customers and how to stop disturbances.

Handling a guest who has had too much to drink can be a bartender's most difficult job. The drunken customer may cause a scene, make other guests uncomfortable, ruin the atmosphere, cause physical harm to other guests, or damage property. It must be remembered that the person who has had too much to drink is neither reasonable nor rational. The bar becomes liable for his or her actions, and it is the bartender's responsibility to protect other guests and the owner's property. In no instance should the bartender resort to physical force or be verbally abusive to a guest. When management is on the premises, the bartender should notify them and let them solve the problem. If the bartender must handle it alone, he or she should be firm and insist that the person leave the premises. If the guest is too drunk to drive, the bartender should arrange for another driver. When the bartender cannot handle the problem, the police should be called in. A good bartender should be able to control the bar and its guests. He or she should also be able to refuse service to the inebriated customer.

The bartender must be a good listener, but never offer advice. A good bartender anticipates a customer's needs but never forces additional sales. At all times, he or she must be in complete control of the bar.

## CLOSING

At the end of a work shift, the bartender goes through the closing procedures, which are as important as opening ones. His or her major responsibility is accounting for the beverages sold. The bartender counts the contents of the cash register, deducts the opening bank, and makes out and turns in his or her deposit. In an establishment that has sophisticated electronic cash registers, a reading of the machine may be required. In many bars, part of the closing procedure entails taking inventory of the remaining stock. If the bar uses metered bottles, it is relatively easy to record the closing figures from the meters. When the bar does not utilize metered bottles, the bartender must take a sight inventory of all bottles and record the count as tenths of bottles. All bar equipment must be cleaned and the sinks emptied, all ashtrays washed and garbage removed. A bar that is not cleaned nightly rapidly deteriorates and picks up objectionable odors.

The last duty in closing is checking for fire hazards and the security of the bar.

### Review and Discussion Questions

1. Describe the bartender's duties.
2. Discuss the three basic types of mixed drinks, with emphasis on the method of preparation.
3. Explain the need for beverage control, and describe the various methods employed.
4. Discuss the problems the bartender might encounter in handling guests.
5. List the bartender's closing duties.

# Beverage
# Control
# Through
# Standards

**Objectives**

This chapter is designed to acquaint the student with beverage control through the implementation of standards. The student, after studying this chapter, should be able to:

1. Discuss systems and standards of operation for controlling beverages for profitable bar operation.

2. Establish a control system for an operating bar.

3. Understand standard pricing and percentages.

4. Recognize standard methods of operation that are acceptable in the beverage industry.

**13**

Profit is not a dirty word! It is basic to any business, but it requires planning. Beverage control is the beverage industry's means of profit planning. We must control the five M's of business (machinery, money, material, manpower, and methods) if we are to be successful. Controls *must* be built into the operation from its very conception. Machinery, or equipment, has been discussed in Chapter 11, and handling money in Chapter 12. This chapter discusses the control of material, manpower, and methods.

## MATERIAL

The flow of material or merchandise (beverage) must be controlled from purchase to dispensing. Before a commodity can be purchased, a need for it must be established. It is management's responsibility to decide the type of beverage to be used, from whom it is to be purchased, and in what quantity. In a large operation, management may turn this responsibility over to a food and beverage manager or purchasing steward. In no case, however, should this be delegated to the employee operating the bar. One of the cardinal rules in any beverage operation is that all work and responsibility within the beverage department must be divided to reduce the opportunity for theft.

## MANPOWER

In controlling manpower, we are concerned with selecting, training, and scheduling beverage employees. In the hiring process, job descriptions (see job description table in this chapter) and a training program must be provided to familiarize new employees with the establishment's standards. References must be checked and new employees bonded. Before new employees are allowed to be on their own, they should work with seasoned employees to get accustomed to the methods and responsibilities of the job. In scheduling employees, peak periods must be taken into consideration and job analysis used for upgrading employee efficiency.

## METHOD

It is management's responsibility to establish systems and standards of operation to control methods. Standards are built into the system to ensure that the customer is always receiving a perfect drink at a fair price, and ownership is receiving a fair return of its investment. Employees must be made aware of the standards, and management must enforce them. To control any operation, the folllowing standards should be set up for the bar:

1. Standard drink list (menu) with fixed prices,
2. Standard recipes,
3. Standard pricing policy,
4. Standard brands, and
5. Standard methods of operation.

### Standard Drink List

To establish a standard drink list, the type of bar and its clientele should be taken into consideration. In a tavern, with little or no food business, it would be foolish to stock a large inventory of vintage wines; and conversely, if in a high-priced cocktail lounge, the less expensive brands would not be carried. Management must predetermine the types of clientele it is going to cater to, the types of beverages that customers are accustomed to drinking, and in what quantity. The bartender should be prepared to make almost any drink, but the inventory should be in accordance with the establishment's needs. Unless there is a delivery problem, no beverage establishment should inventory more than a thirty-day supply of merchandise, with the exception of vintage wines. It costs money to warehouse, or inventory, merchandise that doesn't turn over, and there is no return on capital invested in unused merchandise. Inventory also ties up space and presents an opportunity for breakage or theft. A rule of thumb is that inventory on the shelf costs a minimum of 1 percent a month. One should keep in mind that nothing is a "good buy" unless there is an established need for it.

## Standard Recipes

Standard recipes are established so that every drink is uniform. The customer can be assured of consistency in taste, amount of alcohol, and method of preparation. Standard recipes are written only after experimenting with formulas and taste testing by selected customers. Does the customer require a 1-, 1½-, or 2-ounce drink? A customer survey should be conducted before standard recipes are established.

Once the recipes have been established, the bartender must be trained in using them. The bartender should also be given some latitude in satisfying customers' wishes. The bar should be flexible enough to accommodate the customer who wants a 10-to-1 Martini or no garnish in an Old Fashioned. Chapter 16 includes standard drink recipes which are used in a national hotel chain. The chain found customer acceptance was high; but even more important, customers were assured of the same high-quality drink at all chain locations across the United States.

## Standard Pricing

Standard pricing means charging every customer the same price, with no discount to favored guests. This is simple to accomplish; however, a standard markup must be established first to ensure a reasonable profit. This must be decided by management, put into effect, and reviewed periodically as costs increase.

There is no industry-wide standard percentage of markup. The individual bar owner must establish a formula based on a desired percentage of return on investment. For example: a full quart contains 32 ounces. If a bottle of Scotch cost $6.40, it would then cost $.20 per ounce. In a 1½-ounce Scotch Highball, the beverage cost would be $.30. There are other costs involved: the club soda, bartender's salary, overhead, etc. Taking a fixed amount for these surrounding costs (in this example, $.05 per drink), the total cost can be set at $.35 for the Scotch Highball. Next, the percentage of beverage cost that is desired must be predetermined. For a beverage cost of 25 percent, multiply the $.35 by 400 percent, and the drink price would be $1.40.

Generally, for pricing and inventory control, beverages are divided into four categories: 1) wines, 2) beers, 3) distilled spirits, and 4) nonalcoholic beverages. In many establishments, wine and beer have a lower percentage of markup then the distilled spirits, and nonalcoholic beverages higher.

Based on the percentage of each category sold, management should establish an overall beverage cost percentage. The day of estimating cost, and just charging what the traffic will bear, has ended. Today, all the tools of modern management must be utilized and the actual cost for overhead, salaries, etc., known. The operation must be programmed for success, not left to chance. It is important that management establish a price for every product to be sold and not deviate from it.

## Standard Brands

The case for using standard brands is strong. It is one of the best methods that I know for controlling inventory and at the same time providing customers with a choice of quality. If the operator has selected Seagram Seven Crown for the bar whiskey, and the patrons become accustomed to Manhattans being made with it, they are not going to be receptive to the management replacing it with a whiskey of lesser quality because it was on sale this month. Recipes are designed to please customers and produce a profit. Without standard brands, there can be no standard recipes.

There are many distillers, wineries, and brewers that want business. It is up to management to make the selection. Certainly, owners can't afford to have every brand that is available on the market represented at their bars. The brands and variety of spirits that are regularly called for by patrons should be carried on inventory in the amount that will turn over once a month.

## Standard Methods of Operation

Standard methods of operation is a systematic approach to managing a beverage facility. Planning is the key to a successful operation. Standard operating procedures are the means of obtaining continuity of quality and service within the establishment. Employees must be trained in the how and why of the bar's operation. Guidelines must be set up so the individual employee always performs to established standards. Policies concerning hours of operation, credit, and merchandising should be enforced by management's representative, the bartender, uniformly to all customers at all times.

## JOB DESCRIPTION

**Job Title:** Bartender

**Salary Range:** Entry level _____ Maximum _____

**Experience Required:** _____

**Education Level:** High school graduate

**Additional Education:** Graduate of professional bartending school

**Physical Ability:**
1) Be able to work standing up for extended lengths of time.
2) Be able to lift up to 75 pounds.
3) Be able to follow directions.
4) Be able to do simple math.

**Personality:**
1) Be friendly.
2) Be a good communicator.

**Other:** Must be bondable.

**Duties:**
A. Be responsible for the cleanliness of the bar and lounge area.
   1) Fill sink with fresh water, detergent, and antibacterial agent.
   2) Polish bar top and back bar.
   3) Put out clean ashtrays and cocktail napkins.
B. Replenish supplies.
   1) Requisition from storeroom necessary beverages to bring inventory to par stock level.
   2) Requisition from kitchen fresh fruit and fruit juices for garnish tray.
   3) Check $CO_2$ unit on draught beer unit and premix unit.
   4) Fill ice bins.
C. Cut fresh fruit for garnish and prepare juices.
D. Maintain control system.
   1) Take beginning inventory of beverage store.
   2) Draw operating bank with sufficient change for shift.
   3) Draw sufficient guest checks and check and verify the sequence of numbers.

4) Make sure the cash register is cleared and has a supply of recording tape.

E. Provide services.

1) Prepare all requested drinks with standard recipes and ring up all transactions on cash register.

2) Maintain discipline in bar.

F. Perform end of shift tasks.

1) Clean bar area and empty sinks.

2) Remove garbage.

3) Inventory beverage.

4) Ring out cash register.

G. Make turn-in.

1) Process receipts.

2) Account for guest checks, both used and unused.

3) Deposit bank.

4) Clear cash register.

5) Lock bar.

H. Perform checkout tasks.

1) Remove all ashtrays to kitchen.

2) Check all locks and the security of barroom.

3) Inspect for possible fire hazards.

---

## Review and Discussion Questions

1. Discuss management's responsibility in the control of a beverage operation.

2. What are the five standards management should be aware of to effectively control a beverage operation?

3. Using a 1½-ounce standard for measurement, establish a retail price for a highball with a wholesale price per 32-ounce bottle at $7.20, a desired percentage of beverage cost at 25 percent, and at $.10 surround cost.

4. Why is it important for management to establish standard brands for bar whiskey?

# Purchasing, Receiving, Storing, and Issuing of Beverages

**Objectives**

This chapter discusses the control of beverages from purchasing to issuing. The student, after studying this chapter should be able to:

1. Discuss management's responsibility in purchasing alcoholic beverages.

2. Design a control system, including receiving, inventorying, and issuing alcoholic beverages.

3. Recognize the need for security and control of beverages between purchasing and issuing.

# 14

Controlling the flow of beverage is one of the beverage manager's major responsibilities. The need for a commodity must be established; then a control system must be designed to protect and account for the beverages used. It has been established that the reason for operating a business is to make a profit, and unless expenses are controlled, the profit needed to give an adequate return on the owner's investment cannot be guaranteed.

## PURCHASING

Control of purchasing therefore becomes a major factor in beverage management. Costs are analyzed on a regular basis with the use of a profit and loss statement or a monthly operating report.

It is management's responsibility to determine what brands are to be used, the number of varieties to be stocked, and the quantity to be carried on inventory. Customer preference, availability of supply, and monthly turnover must be taken into consideration.

In selecting wholesalers (nonmonopoly states), management will take into consideration the product line, credit terms, delivery schedules, and prices, when not regulated by the state. Friendship with a particular salesperson should not be the main factor in selecting the wholesaler. Once the brands and the wholesaler have been selected, the weekly ordering of beverage is accomplished by checking inventory and anticipating needs for the ordering period.

# RECEIVING

As mentioned in Chapter 13, responsibility in the beverage department should be divided. The person doing the purchasing should not do the receiving. The person doing the receiving should have the same accountability as the purchaser. Purchase orders should be checked against the bill of lading, condition of the merchandise verified, and an actual count taken. At no time should the beverage be out of sight or control of the person receiving it.

# STORING

Once the beverage is received, it should be placed on inventory and securely locked in the storage area. There are two approaches to valuation at this point. The traditional one is inventory at cost; the newer approach is inventory at sales value. There are advantages to both systems. The first gives a true value of cost, but doesn't reflect replacement value or sales value, as does the second system. There are many inventory systems including bin cards, monthly verification count, and running inventory. Some are based on numerical count, others on a dollar valuation. The beverages should always be stored in a safe location under lock and key, and no one other than the beverage steward should have access to them.

# ISSUING

The issuing process may be controlled in several ways. The head bartender should requisition replacement needs at the beginning of each shift with the return of empty bottles. Standard issuing hours should be established, and all requisitions must be time and date stamped. A requisition should be signed by the beverage manager or head bartender.

To understand the complete system more readily, let us trace a specific item through the system. Management has decided the bar bourbon will be Old Crow. The bartender estimates that during the period of a month the bar will use five cases of quarts.

The purchasing steward places an order with the ABC wholesale house for five cases of Old Crow to be delivered on June 1, at a price of $5.00 per quart, or $60 per case. The steward issues a purchase order for the ABC Company, with a copy for the receiving room, and a copy is retained in the office (see Example 1).

*Example 1*

## PURCHASE ORDER

Company: <u>ABC</u>                                      Order # <u>1</u>
                                                          Date: <u>June 1</u>

| ITEM | SIZE | QUANTITY | PRICE | EXTENSION |
|---|---|---|---|---|
| Old Crow | Quart | 5 cases | $60.00 | $300.00 |
| | | | Total | $300.00 |

Authorized Signature _____

When the ABC Company delivers the five cases of Old Crow on June 1, the receiving clerk checks the bill of lading against the purchase order. If they agree, the clerk signs for the five cases, enters them on a daily receiving sheet (see Example 2), and locks them in the storage room.

*Example 2*

## DAILY RECEIVING SCHEDULE

| ITEM | QUANTITY | COUNT | PRICE | CONDITION | TIME |
|---|---|---|---|---|---|
| Old Crow | 5 cases | 12 quarts | $60 | OK | 1 p.m. |

Receiving clerk's signature: _____

Once the Old Crow is in the storeroom, it is recorded on an inventory card (see Example 3).

*Example 3*

### INVENTORY CONTROL CARD

| ITEM | IN | DATE | OUT | ON HAND |
|------|-----|------|-----|---------|
| Old Crow | 60 quarts | June 1 | | 60 quarts |

It will remain in the storeroom until it is requisitioned by the bartender for use at the bar. The bartender returns empty bottles for full ones, along with a requisition request (see Example 4).

*Example 4*

### REQUISITION REQUEST

Location: Front Bar          Date:   June 2
                                         Time:

| ITEM | SIZE | QUANTITY |
|------|------|----------|
| Old Crow | Quart | 5 cases |

Bartender's signature _____

Storeroom attendant's signature _____

Once the beverage (in this case, the Old Crow) reaches the bar, control is established in dispensing it by standard drink recipes, use of measured shots, or preset dispensing units, as explained in Chapter 12. No matter what measuring system is used, a standard measured drink portion is the basis of any bar control system.

Any system of control will only be as good as the employees involved in it. Management must concern itself with the selection of qualified personnel for the storeroom area.

The sale of the beverage must be accounted for; this is done by two methods: 1) use of a cash register that has a printed tape and 2) a visual inventory, made by the bartender at the end of his or her shift (see Chapter 12). If there is control over the flow of beverage from purchasing to accounting, there is less chance of theft, and a profit will be generated.

### Review and Discussion Questions

1. Discuss management's responsibility in the purchase of alcoholic beverages.
2. What must be taken into consideration when selecting a wholesaler?
3. Describe the difference between:
   a) daily receiving schedule,
   b) requisition request, and
   c) purchase order.
4. How does the bartender replace depleted stock?

# Beverage Law

## Objectives

This chapter is designed to introduce the reader to state and federal laws involved in operating an alcoholic beverage establishment. The student, after studying this chapter, should be able to:

1. Explain the state's role in licensing bars.

2. Analyze the protection to the public provided by federal laws regarding the sale of alcoholic beverages.

3. Describe practices that are illegal, under state and federal laws, concerning the handling of alcoholic beverages.

# 15

A beverage license may be defined as a privilege granted to a qualified person by a lawfully constituted authority, permitting the holder to engage in business under certain conditions and with certain restrictions. The licensee should accept this privilege with the knowledge that he or she is expected to operate in a certain manner and to obey all of the laws and regulations pertaining to alcoholic beverages. A license to operate a bar is, therefore, a precious commodity and should be protected at all times. If it is withdrawn, the business cannot operate.

Licensing is controlled by local government; however, state and federal laws apply to the operation of bars. When in doubt, an operator should consult the local Alcoholic Beverage Control (ABC) office and seek advice from a good lawyer who is familiar with beverage law.

## FEDERAL LAWS

The federal government exercises control over the alcoholic beverage industry in two major areas:

1. Protection of tax revenues.
2. Protection of the public from adulterated or mishandled goods.

The beverage industry must also comply with all laws that govern all businesses.

The federal government exercises its authority through:

1. The Food and Drug Administration of the United States Department of Agriculture.
2. The Alcohol and Tobacco Division of the Treasury Department.
3. The Federal Trade Commission.

The Department of Agriculture and the Federal Trade Commission are mainly concerned with consumer protection, whereas, the Treasury Department is concerned with the protection of tax monies to which the federal government is entitled. The Alcohol and Tobacco Tax Division (ATTD) issues licenses to producers, approves labeling and advertising, and supervises trade practices. Both divisions employ inspectors who may enter the premises at any time for inspection to ensure that federal laws are not being broken.

Before any licensee may sell any alcoholic beverage, he or she must possess a tax stamp issued by the federal government. Tax stamps are not a license to do business, and a state license is required before any beverage may be sold in the state.

## STATE LAWS

State laws and controls vary. There are three major types of state options:

*Monopoly states*: these states control the sale of distilled spirits and certain kinds of wine through the operation of their own state liquor stores. In many cases they would be called "dry states," in that there were no open bars dispensing mixed drinks up until 1978. North Carolina is an example of this type of state control.

*Control states*: these states control the sale of all alcoholic beverages distributed in their territories. They may have open bars, as in Pennsylvania, or be dry states.

*Open license states:* private business makes both on-premise and off-premise sales of alcoholic beverages to all types of consumers. Each state sets its own licensing policy, and they differ widely. An example of an open license state is New York.

## The Dram Shop Act

One law that will be found in all states, in some form or another, prohibits the sale of alcoholic beverages to intoxicated persons. Illegal sales to intoxicated persons may prove very costly to the licensee involved. The law states that if an intoxicated person injures another person or damages property, then the licensee who furnished him with any part of the beverage consumed, may be held liable to the injured party in the same degree as the intoxicated person. In some states this law is referred to as the Dram Shop Act. Dram shop insurance may be purchased to cover the establishment; however, it is extremely costly.

## LOCAL LAWS

Local government controls the issuing of licenses, location of bars, and hours of operation. Again, rules and regulations vary widely, and the operation should become familiar with local ABC laws. Most communities restrict the number of licenses issued, according to population. They also control location, in that they may prohibit a business being located within 300 feet of a church or school. They also have discretion of to whom they issue a license. Many state and local governments prohibit the issuing of licenses to known criminals (those who have been convicted of a felony), non-U.S. citizens, and nonresidents of the state.

There are many practices that are frowned upon or illegal, and the bartender should be aware of them. Some of these practices are:

1. It is illegal to refill or reuse a liquor bottle. All empty bottles must be broken and the label destroyed.

2. There must be a federal tax stamp on the bottle at all times.

3. It is illegal to offer for sale alcohol purchased in a state other than the one in which it is being sold, unless state tax has been paid on it in the sales state.

4. It is illegal to water or dilute alcoholic beverages in their original containers.

5. In some states, it is illegal to make or sell premixed drinks.

6. Alcoholic beverage licenses must be on public display at all times.

7. In most states, it is illegal to have gambling on the premises.

8. Substitution of one brand for another when a customer has specifically requested one is illegal, unless the customer is informed of the substitution.

9. In many states, all alcoholic beverages must be paid for in cash on receipt of the beverage, with credit not to be extended.

10. Many states have posted wholesale prices and do not allow special sales prices or giveaways.

11. It is illegal to serve minors; the age varies from 18 to 21 years of age.

Bartenders should become familiar with all laws governing the bars in which they are employed. Ignorance of the law is no excuse for breaking it.

## Review and Discussion Questions

1. Discuss the licensee's responsibility in relation to state alcoholic beverage laws.
2. What is the Dram Shop Act and how does it affect the licensee?
3. Compare operation under the three major types of state options.
4. List ten practices that are either frowned upon or illegal in a bar operation.

## Recipes

**Objectives**

This chapter contains the recipes most often encountered by the practicing bartender. The student, after studying this chapter, should be able to:

1. Recognize the major drinks mixed at a commercial bar.

2. Describe the type of glasses used for various mixed drinks.

3. Discuss the importance of using quality ingredients.

**16**

The art of mixing drinks cannot be learned by merely reading about it, any more than gourmet cooking can be learned without being in a kitchen and practicing the profession.

This chapter introduces basic mixing rules and standard recipes used in one hotel chain. There are variations for every recipe, and each establishment has its own standards. The bartender should comply with the standards of his place of employment, give the customer an honest drink, accurately measured, well prepared, and properly garnished.

## INGREDIENTS

A drink is only as good as the sum total of its ingredients. The proper garnish is as important as the alcohol for flavor, appearance, and color. Mixes and juices must be fresh and of good quality.

Ice is also important. It should be of the type called for in the recipe, and fresh ice should always be used for every drink. The ice should always be placed in the glass first, so that all ingredients will be properly chilled and splashing will be reduced.

Sugar also plays an important part in mixology. Sugar does not dissolve readily in alcohol; therefore, it must be mixed with either water or fruit juice before the spirits are added to the drink.

# METHODS

Drinks that are to be stirred should be stirred briskly, but only enough to thoroughly mix and chill the drink. Shake drinks should be shaken vigorously, but not long enough to dilute the drink more than is required for perfect blending. Remember that wine bruises easily and should never be shaken in a drink. Fruit garnishes should be cut properly and covered so that they will not dry out or attract fruit flies.

If the bartender does not know how to make a drink requested by a customer, he or she should ask how the customer prefers it to be made or look it up in a bartender's guide. If the proper ingredients are not available, no substitutions should be made without the patron's permission.

# GLASSES

The proper glass helps to make a drink much more attractive. Listed below are the glasses most commonly found in commercial bars.

*Jigger, whiskey jigger, or shot glass*: a small glass that holds 1½ ounces

*Cocktail glass*: a funnel-shaped, stemmed glass that holds 4½ ounces

*Old Fashioned glass*: a low, squat glass that holds 4 to 6 ounces

*Cordial glass*: slender, tulip-shaped, stemmed glass that holds 1 ounce

*Champagne glass*: a wide-mouthed, tulip-shaped, stemmed glass that holds 5 or 6 ounces

*Whiskey Sour glass or sour glass*: a short-stemmed, slender, tulip-shaped glass that holds 4 to 6 ounces

*Highball glass*: a medium-size, straight-sided glass that holds between 5 and 8 ounces

*Brandy snifter*: a large balloon-shaped glass. The two most common sizes are 8 ounce and 12 ounce

*Collins glass*: a tall, straight-sided, frosted glass that can hold 10 to 12 ounces of the flavor

The following are wine glasses that may be used to ensure full flavor and guest satisfaction.

*Champagne glass:* a wide-mouthed, tall, tulip-shaped, stemmed glass that holds 5 to 6 ounces

*Wine glass:* a short-stemmed, tall, tubular glass that will hold 8 to 10 ounces

*Sherry glass:* a short-stemmed, tulip-shaped glass that serves 5 to 6 ounces

*Balloon snifter:* a large, balloon-shaped glass that will hold 8 to 10 ounces

On the following five pages are drink recipes utilized in a hotel chain recognized for quality drinks.

## BRANDY, CORDIAL, AND OTHER DRINKS

| Drink | Ingredients | Ice | Method | Glass | Garnish |
|---|---|---|---|---|---|
| Jack Rose | 1½ oz. apple jack<br>½ oz. lime juice<br>1 tsp. grenadine | cubed | Shake and strain. | cocktail | lime slice |
| Margarita | 1 oz. tequila<br>¼ oz. Triple Sec<br>½ oz. lime juice | cubed | Shake and strain. | cocktail | salted rim |
| Side Car | 1 oz. brandy<br>½ oz. Triple Sec<br>½ oz. lemon juice | cubed | Shake and strain. | cocktail | sugared rim |
| Stinger | 1 oz. brandy<br>1 oz. creme de menthe, white | cubed | Shake and strain. | cocktail | |
| Brandy Alexander | 1 oz. brandy<br>½ oz. creme de cacao<br>½ oz. heavy cream | cubed | Shake and strain. | champagne | dash of nutmeg |
| Grasshopper | ¾ oz. green creme de menthe<br>¾ oz. white creme de cacao<br>¾ oz. heavy cream | cubed | Shake and strain. | champagne | |
| Sloe Gin Fizz | ¾ oz. lemon juice<br>1 tsp. sugar<br>1½ oz. sloe gin<br>club soda | cubed | Mix lemon, sugar, and sloe gin over ice. Top with club soda. | highball | |
| Pink Squirrel | 1 oz. creme de almond<br>½ oz. creme de cacao, white<br>1 oz. heavy cream | cubed | Shake and strain. | champagne | |
| French 75 | 1½ oz. brandy<br>1 oz. lemon juice<br>1 tsp. sugar<br>Split of champagne | cubed | Place ice in glass. Pour in lemon juice, sugar, and brandy. Top with champagne. | highball | lemon slices |

## VODKA DRINKS

| Drink | Ingredients | Ice | Method | Glass | Garnish |
|---|---|---|---|---|---|
| **Bloody Mary** | 1½ oz. vodka<br>3 oz. tomato juice<br>½ oz. lemon juice<br>2 dashes Worcester-<br>shire sauce<br>1 dash hot pepper<br>Salt and pepper | cubed | Shake and strain.<br>Pour over cubed<br>ice. | highball | celery<br>stalk |
| **Screwdriver** | 1½ oz. vodka<br>4 oz. orange juice | cubed | Put ice in glass<br>and pour ingredi-<br>ents over ice. | highball | orange<br>slices |
| **Black Russian** | 1½ oz. vodka<br>½ oz. coffee<br>liqueur | crushed | Stir and strain. | cocktail | |
| **Bull Shot** | 1½ oz. vodka<br>4 oz. beef bouillon | cubed | Pour over ice. | rock<br>glass | |
| **Harvey Wallbanger** | 1½ oz. vodka<br>½ oz. Galliano<br>3 oz. orange juice | cubed | Pour orange juice<br>and vodka over<br>ice. Float<br>Galliano. | collins | |
| **Moscow Mule** | 1½ oz. vodka<br>½ oz. lime juice<br>ginger beer | cubed | Mix over ice. | 8-oz.<br>copper<br>mug | lime slice |

## RUM DRINKS

| Drink | Ingredients | Ice | Method | Glass | Garnish |
|---|---|---|---|---|---|
| Daiquiri | 1½ oz. light rum<br>½ oz. lime juice<br>½ oz. simple syrup | cubed | Shake and strain. | cocktail or champagne | lime slice |
| Bacardi | 1½ oz. light rum<br>½ oz. lime juice<br>¼ oz. grenadine<br>¼ oz. simple syrup | cubed | Shake and strain. | cocktail or champagne | lime slice |
| Mai Tai | 1½ oz. rum<br>½ tsp. sugar<br>½ oz. orange curacao<br>½ oz. grenadine<br>½ oz. lime juice | cubed | Shake and strain. | rock glass | pineapple slice and cherry |
| Hot Buttered Rum | 1½ oz. Jamaica rum<br>5 oz. hot water<br>1 pat butter | | Pour water and add rum to mug. Float butter pat. | 8-oz. mug | cinnamon stick and dash nutmeg |
| Planter's Punch | 1 oz. light rum<br>½ oz. dark rum<br>½ oz. Falernum<br>1 oz. lime juice<br>1 tsp. sugar | cubed | Shake light rum, Falernum, lime juice, and sugar. Strain and serve with cubed ice. Float dark rum on top. | collins | pineapple slice, orange slice, and cherry |

# GIN DRINKS

| Drink | Ingredients | Ice | Method | Glass | Garnish |
|---|---|---|---|---|---|
| Martini | 1½ oz. gin<br>¼ oz. dry vermouth | crushed | Stir and strain. | cocktail | olive or<br>lemon peel |
| Gibson | 1½ oz. gin<br>⅛ oz. dry vermouth | crushed | Stir and strain. | cocktail | cocktail<br>onion |
| Dubonnet | 1 oz. gin<br>1 oz. Dubonnet | crushed | Stir and strain. | cocktail | lemon peel |
| Gimlet | 1½ oz. gin<br>½ oz. lime juice | crushed | Stir and strain. | cocktail | lime slice |
| Singapore Sling | 2 oz. gin<br>1 oz. cherry liqueur<br>1 oz. lime juice | cubed | Shake and strain. | highball | 4 drops<br>Benedictine,<br>4 drops<br>brandy,<br>orange slice,<br>fresh mint |
| Bronx | 1 oz. gin<br>½ oz. sweet ver-<br>mouth<br>½ oz. dry vermouth<br>½ oz. orange juice | cubed | Shake and strain. | cocktail | orange slice |
| Tom Collins | 1½ oz. gin<br>1 oz. lemon juice<br>½ oz. simple syrup<br>3 oz. club soda | cubed | Place ice in glass.<br>Add all ingredi-<br>ents. Top with<br>club soda. Stir. | collins | orange slice<br>and cherry |
| Alexander | 1 oz. gin<br>½ oz. creme de cacao<br>½ oz. heavy cream | cubed | Shake and strain. | champagne | dash of<br>nutmeg |
| Perfect | 1¼ oz. gin<br>¼ oz. dry vermouth<br>¼ oz. sweet ver-<br>mouth<br>1 dash bitters | crushed | Stir and strain. | cocktail | lemon peel |
| Pink Lady | 1 oz. gin<br>1½ oz. heavy cream<br>½ oz. grenadine | crushed | Shake and strain. | champagne | |

## WHISKEY DRINKS

| Drink | Ingredients | Ice | Method | Glass | Garnish |
|---|---|---|---|---|---|
| Old Fashioned | 1½ oz. whiskey<br>1 tsp. sugar<br>3 dashes bitters<br>1 oz. club soda | cubed | Muddle sugar, bitters, and soda. Add ice, then whiskey. | Old Fashioned or rock glass | orange slices |
| Manhattan | 1½ oz. whiskey<br>¾ oz. sweet vermouth | crushed | Stir and strain. | cocktail | cherry |
| Dry Manhattan | 1½ oz. whiskey<br>¾ oz. dry vermouth | crushed | Stir and strain. | cocktail | lemon peel or olive |
| Rob Roy | 1½ oz. Scotch whiskey<br>¾ oz. sweet vermouth | crushed | Stir and strain. | cocktail | cherry |
| Whiskey Sour | 1½ oz. whiskey<br>1 oz. lemon juice | crushed | Shake and strain. | Whiskey Sour | orange slices and cherry |
| John Collins | 1½ oz. whiskey<br>1 oz. lemon juice<br>½ oz. simple syrup<br>3 oz. club soda | cubed | Place ice in glass. Add all ingredients, top with club soda, and stir. | collins | orange slices and cherry |
| Mint Julep | 2 oz. bourbon<br>1 tsp. sugar<br>Mint leaves<br>2 tbsp. water | shaved | Muddle mint, water, and sugar. Pack glass with shaved ice and pour in bourbon. | chilled 12-oz. pewter cup or glass | fresh mint |
| Rusty Nail | 1¼ oz. Scotch<br>½ oz. Drambuie | cubed | Stir in glass. | Old Fashioned or rocks | |
| Irish Coffee | 1½ oz. Irish whiskey<br>5 oz. black coffee<br>1 tsp. sugar<br>Sweet whipped cream | | Pour coffee in mug. Float whiskey, then add whipped cream. | 8-oz. stemmed goblet | |

**Review and Discussion Questions**

1. List the important considerations in mixing any drink.
2. Describe the types of glasses that may be found at a quality bar.
3. Why is the use of quality ingredients important in mixing drinks?

# Glossary

*alcohol:*  A colorless, volatile liquid ($C_2H_5OH$), formed from certain sugars by fermentation.

*amontillado:*  A dry, pale to light gold sherry from Spain.

*Amoroso:*  A medium-dry, golden sherry from Spain.

*aperitif:*  A wine designed to whet the appetite.

*aqua vitae:*  A Latin phrase meaning "water of life." A spirituous liquor.

*aroma:*  A wine's or spirit's odor or bouquet.

*Auslese:*  (*Aus* meaning selected; *lese* meaning picking). A German wine made from sorted and selected grapes.

*Beerenauslese:*  (Selected berry picking) A German wine made from selected overripe grapes.

*bianco:*  The Italian word for "white."

*blanco:*  The Spanish word for "white."

*blending:*  Mixing products of various sorts or grades to obtain a particular kind or quality.

*Bocksbeutel:*  The German wine, Steinwein, is traditionally sold in this squat, flasklike bottle.

*body:*  Consistency or density; substance; strength as opposed to thinness (for example, wine of a good body).

*botanicals:*  Flavoring materials, such as juniper, orris root, anise, lemon, etc., used to impart flavor nuances to gin.

*bottled in bond:*  Straight whiskeys, distilled at not more than 160 proof, four years old or more, bottled at 100 proof. Does not imply quality; has reference only to the internal revenue tax.

*bouquet:*  The characteristic aroma of wines, liqueurs, etc.

*brut:*  A word used to describe very dry wines (usually champagne).

*call liquor:*   That liquor, stocked in a bar, that the customer orders by brand name.

*cask:*   A barrel-like container made of staves (usually oak) for holding wines or spirits.

*catalysis:*   The causing of a chemical change by adding a substance (the catalyst) that is not affected by the reaction.

*cellar:*   A room, usually underground, used for storing wine.

*chateau:*   One of the more than 4000 vineyards in the Bordeaux region of France, where wine is produced from the grapes grown at the particular vineyard or estate.

*crusted:*   A port not up to the standard of vintage port. Has a dark ruby color and a good fruity bouquet.

*decanter:*   A bottle, usually ornamental, from which wines or spirits are served at the table.

*demi:*   A French word meaning "half."

*demi sec:*   A French term meaning "half-dry," describing a quite sweet champagne.

*distillation:*   The obtaining of the essence or volatile properties of a substance.

*doux:*   A French word meaning "sweet"; usually used to describe a very sweet champagne.

*Dram Shop Act:*   A law holding the licensed seller of beverages liable for the damaging acts of an intoxicated customer.

*dry:*   The opposite of sweet. Lacking in sugar. A dry champagne would be medium sweet.

*ethyl alcohol:*   (*See:* Alcohol) The principal alcohol found in alcoholic beverages.

*extra sec:*   Describes a dry champagne.

*fermentation:*   A change brought about by a ferment, such as yeast enzymes which convert grape sugar into ethyl alcohol, etc.

*Fino:*   A very pale, dry, sturdy-bodied Spanish sherry.

*fortified:*   Wines that are fortified will have alcohol added in the form of brandy.

*fruity:*   A very definite grape taste found in better wines.

*Genever:*   A full-flavored gin with a malty aroma and taste.

*jeroboam:*   A large champagne bottle holding 104 ounces.

*lagering:*   A maturing period in which beer is stored for aging and dissipation of cloudiness.

*liqueur:*   (Cordial) An alcoholic beverage made by combining a spirit with flavoring, then adding sugar syrup in excess of 2½ percent of the volume.

*magnum:*   A champagne bottle holding 52 ounces.

*malt:*   A germinated grain used in brewing and distilling.

*mash:*   Crushed malt or meal of grain mixed with hot water to form wort.

*mead:*   An alcoholic liquor made by fermenting honey and water.

*monopole:*   A private brand label used on wine from the Bordeaux region.

*Oloroso:*   A sherry from Spain. A deep golden wine, sweet but still dry, full-bodied, heavy nutty flavor.

*over proof:*   Alcoholic strength is over 100 proof.

*pasteurization:*   Sterilization and killing of yeast. Takes place at 140 to 145°F.

*patent still:*   (Coffey still) A continuous or two-column still.

*Pedro Ximenez:*   (P.X.) A grape variety used for making very sweet wines and for blended sherries.

*pony:*   A glass holding 1 liquid ounce.

*pot still:*   A copper pot with a broad, rounded bottom and a long tapered neck, which is connected to a worm condenser.

*proof:*   The alcoholic strength of a liquid. Each degree of proof equals 0.5 percent of alcohol.

*rectifying:*   Changing the natural state of a spirit, such as flavoring dry gin with the oils of a specific fruit.

*reducing:*   Adding water to lower alcoholic strength.

*rocks:*   A glass holding 8 ounces. Also called an Old Fashioned glass.

*rosado:*   A Spanish rose wine.

*ruby:*   A young, deep red port.

*Schnapps:*   A German word meaning "spirituous liquor."

*sec:*   A French word meaning "dry."

*shell:*   An 8- to 10-ounce glass for beer.

*snifter:*   A 5-ounce glass for brandy.

*Solera system:*   A constant process of blending sherry.

*spatlese:*   A sweet German wine made from late-picked grapes.

*spirit:*   An alcoholic beverage obtained by distilling out the essence of an alcohol-containing liquid.

*still:*   (*See* pot still and patent still) An apparatus used to distill most spirits.

*tawny:*   A pale, golden port.

*tinto:*   The Spanish word for "red."

*trocken:*   The German word for "dry."

*Trockenbeerenauslese:*   A German wine made from overripe grapes that are attacked by the mold of edelfaule.

*underproof:*   A spirit of less than 100 proof.

*vin:*   The French word for "wine."

*vino:*   The Italian and Spanish word for "wine."

*vintage:*   Indicates the year when a wine is made; the wine from a particular harvest or crop.

*Wein:*   The German word for "wine."

*well liquor:*   (Bar liquor) The liquor used in a bar for the average mixed drink; not ordered by name.

*wort:*   The unfermented or fermenting infusion of malt, which after fermentation becomes beer or mash.

*yeast:*   A plant organism used to induce fermentation in the manufacture of alcoholic liquors.

# Index

Acceptance, customer, 105, 106, 121, 129
Aging of whiskey, 52
Agriculture Department. *See* FDA
Akvavit. *See* Aquavit
Alcohol, 155, 156
Alcohol and Tobacco Tax Division (ATTD), 138
Alcoholic Beverage Control (ABC), 137, 139
Ale, 4, 20
American whiskeys, 47–50
American wines, 27–30
Amontillado, 38, 155
Amoroso, 38, 155
Anisette, 81
Aquavit, 5
Aqua vitae, 155. *See also* Aquavit
Arak, 65
Argentina, wines of, 43
Armagnac, 73
Aroma, 155
Aromatic rum, 65
Assyrians, 3
Atmosphere, 99
Auslese, 37, 155

Babylonians, 3
Balthazar, 34
B and B, 81
Bank, bartender's, 101, 115
Barbados rum, 64, 65
Bar, controlling, 113–114
Barley, 15, 16, 48, 51
Bar liquor. *See* Well liquor
Bar setup, 87–96
Bartender, 87, 91, 99–106, 113–114, 140
    job description, 124–125
Bavarian (beer), 20
Beer, 4, 15–21, 48, 57, 122
Beerenauslese, 37, 155
Benedictine, 81
Beverage flow control, 105, 119–125
Bianco, 155
Blanco, 155
Blended whiskey, 48, 155
Bock beer, 20
Bocksbeutel, 155
Body, 155
Bordeaux wines, 31
Botanicals, 58, 79, 155

Bottled in bond, 50, 155
Bouquet, 155
Bourbon whiskey, 48–49
Brands, standard, 123
Brandy, 26, 73–76, 148
Bread, 4, 15
Brewing process, 17–18
British Guiana rum, 64
Brut, 155

California wines, 27–29
Call liquor, 106, 156
Calvados, 73
Canada
   whiskey, 50
   wines, 42–43
Caramelization, 17
Cash. See Money
   bar, 101
   box, 112
   register, 93, 101, 112–113,
     115, 133
Cask, 156
Cassava, 4
Catalysis, 156
Catering bar, 91–92
Cellar, 156
Champagne bottle sizes, 33–34
Chartreuse, 81
Chateau, 156
Chile, wines of, 43
Circular bar, 89
Cleanup, 115
Closing the bar, 115–116
Cocktail, 5
   lounge, 90–91
Controls, 104–115, 119–125, 132
Control states, 138
Cordials, 4, 79–82, 148
Corn whiskey, 49
Cote d'Or wines, 31–32
Cream, 104
Creme de Cacao, 81
Creme de menthe, 81

Creme de noyaux, 82
Crusted port, 41, 156
Cuban rum, 64
Curacao, 82

Dance floor, 91
Decanter, 156
Demerara rum, 64
Demi, 156
Demi sec, 156
Dionysus, 3
Discipline, 113, 114
Dispensing beer, 18–20
Distillation, 10, 48, 51, 52,
     79–80, 156
Distilled spirits, 122. See also
     Brandy; Cordials; Gin;
     Liqueurs; Rum; Tequila;
     Vodka; Whiskey
Distilled water, 57–58
Doux, 156
Drambuie, 82
Dram Shop Act, 139, 156
Draught beer, 19, 93
Drink list, standard, 120–121,
     148–152
Dry, 156
Dry sink bar, 93

Effects of alcohol, 9
Egg, 104
Egyptians, 3
Electronic control systems,
     106, 115
Emilia, wines of, 35
Equipment, bar, 96
Ethyl alcohol, 156
Extra sec, 156

FDA (Food and Drug
     Administration), 138
Fermentation, 9–10, 156
Fifth, 33
Fino (sherry), 38, 156

Fire hazards, 116
Flavored gin, 58
Fortified wines, 26, 156
France
  brandy, 73–74
  wines, 30–34
Free drinks, 114
Fruit and brandies, 76
Fruit juice. *See* Juices
FTC (Federal Trade
    Commission), 138
Full-bodied rum, 64

Galliano, 82
Garnishes, 90, 94, 101
Genever, 5, 57, 58, 157. *See
    also* Gin
Germany, 5
  wines of, 36–37
Gin, 5, 57–58, 79, 151
Glasses, drinks made in, 102
Glassware, 19, 95, 146–147
Goldwasser, 82
Grains, 9, 16, 47
Grand Marnier, 82
Greece
  brandy, 75
  wines, 44
Guest checks, 101, 112
Guide, bartender's, 102

Half-bottle, 33
Handling, 18–20, 127–133
Happy hour, 112
Herbs. *See* Botanicals
Holland, 5
Hollow square bar, 89
Hops, 15, 16
Horseshoe bar, 88
Hungary, wines of, 42

Ice, 93, 102, 103, 145
Illegal practices, 139–140
Implements, bar, 93–94

Infusion, 80
Ingredients, 145
Inventory, 91, 92, 115, 123, 133
  control card, sample, 132
Ireland, 5
  whiskey, 52
Israel
  brandy, 76
  wines, 44
Issuing, 130–131
Italy
  brandy, 75
  wines, 34–36

Jamaican rum, 64, 65
Java, 65
Jenever. *See* Genever
Jerez, 38
Jeroboam, 34, 157
Juices, 101, 145
Juniper berries, 58

Kahlua, 82
Keg, 18, 20
Koumiss, 4
Kummel, 82

Labeling, wine
  France, 33
  Germany, 36–37
Lager beer, 18, 20, 157
Laws, 114, 137–140
  Federal, 137–138
  local, 139
  state, 138–139
Liability, 115
Licensing, 137
Light-bodied rum, 64
Limited-service bar, 91
Liqueurs, 79–82, 148, 157
Lombardy, wines of, 35

Magnum, 34, 157
Malt, 47, 51, 157

liquor, 20
  whiskey, 49, 51
Management, poor, signs of, 113
Manpower, 119–120
Manual measurement of
  drinks, 105
Maraschino, 82
Marne wines, 32
Mash, 17, 48, 157
Mastikha, 82
Material, 119
Mead, 3, 157
Measurement, beverage, 105–106
Metaxa, 75
Metered bottle system, 105
Methuselah, 34
Mezcal, 70
Michigan wines, 30
Middle Ages, 5
Milk, 104
Mixes, 95, 103
Mixing methods, 102–104, 146
Molasses, 63
Money, 89, 90, 101, 112
Monopole, 157
Monopoly states, 138

Nebuchadnezzar, 34
New York (state) wines, 29
Nonalcoholic beverages, 122

Ohio wines, 30
Old Tom, 57
Oloroso, 38, 157
Open license states, 139
Operation, standard methods of,
  123–125
Ouzo, 75
Overhead, 122
Overproof, 157

Paiwari, 4
Palestinians, 4

Parfait Amour, 82
Pasteurization, 26, 157
Patent still, 157
Peat fire curing, 51
Pedro Ximinez, 157
Percolation, 80
Personal appearance of
  bartender, 100
Peru, brandy of, 75
Piedmont wines, 34
Pilsner, 20
Police, 115
Pony, 157
Port, 5, 41
Porter, 20
Portugal, 5
  brandy of, 75
  wines of, 40–41
Pot still, 157
Preparation of bar, 100–101
Pricing, 92, 104, 112, 122
Profit, 92, 114, 119, 133
Prohibition, 5
Proof, 10, 157
Prunelle, 82
Puerto Rican rum, 64, 65
Pulque, 4
Purchase order, sample, 131
Purchasing, 129

Radio, 114
Receiving, 130
  schedule, sample, 131
Recipes, standard, 121, 145–153
Rectifying, 58, 157
Reducing, 157
Rehoboam, 34
Requisition request, sample, 132
Rhone wines, 33
Rocks, 157
Rosado, 158
Ruby port, 41, 158
Rum, 5, 63–65, 150

Rye whiskey, 49

Sake, 20
St. Gall, monastery of, 4
Salaries, 122
Salmanazar, 34
Sanitation, bar, 100
Schnapps, 158
Scotch whiskey, 50–52
Scotland, 5
Sec, 158
Security of bar, 116
Service bar, 89–90
Service in bar, 101–104
Shake drinks, 102
Shell, 158
Sherry, 5, 38–39
Sicily, wines of, 36
Sloe gin, 82
Snifter, 158
Solera process, 38, 75, 158
Sour mash, 48
South African wines, 43
Spain, 5
    brandy, 74–75
    wines, 37–40
Spatlese, 37, 158
Spirit, 158
Split, 33
Stand-up bar, 87–89
Starch, 9, 48
Still, 11, 47, 51–52, 57, 157, 158
Stirred drinks, 103
Stocking the bar, 100–101
Storage, 130
Stout, 20
Straight-line bar, 88
Strega, 82
Sugar, 9, 25, 48, 63, 79, 145
Sweden, 5
Sweet mash, 48

Tawny port, 41, 158

Television, 114
Temperature,
    of distillation, 10
    of fermentation, 10, 17–18
    of storage, 18, 19
Tequila, 69–70
Theft, 113, 133
Tinto, 158
Tips, 91, 92
Treasury Department. See
    Alcohol and Tobacco Tax
    Division (ATTD)
Trocken, 37, 158
Trockenbeerenauslese, 37, 158
Troubleshooting, beer, 21
Turnover, stock, 123, 129
Tuscany, wines of, 35

Umbria, wines of, 35
Underproof, 158

Venetia, wines of, 35
Vin, 158
Vino, 158
Vintage, 26, 158
Vitis
    labrusca, 25
    vinifera, 25, 26, 27
Vodka, 69, 149
Volume of liquid after
    agitation, 103

Washington (state) wines, 30
Water, 15–16, 57–58, 145
Wein, 158
Weiss beer, 20
Well liquor, 104, 158
Wet bar, 93
Whiskey, 5, 47–52, 152
Wholesalers, 129
Wine, 4, 25–44, 89, 122
    American, 27–30
    French, 30–34

    German, 36–37
    Italian, 34–36
    Portuguese, 40–41
    Spanish, 37–40
Wort, 17, 48, 57, 158

Yeast, 9, 15, 17, 158

Zubrowka, 69